Groovy KITCHEN DESIGNS FOR COLLECTORS

1935-1965

WITH VALUE GUIDE

Schiffer Publishing Ltd

77 Lower Valley Road, Atglen, PA 19310

Michael J. Goldberg

Printed in China

ISBN: 0-7643-0010-5

Book Design by Audrey L. Whiteside

Library of Congress Cataloging-in-Publication Data

Goldberg, Michael J. (Michael Jay)
    Groovy kitchen designs for collectors 1935-1965/ Michael Goldberg.
        p.   cm.
    Includes bibliographical references and index.
    ISBN 0-7643-0010-5 (pbk.)
    1. Kitchen utensils--Collectors and collecting--United States--Catalogs. 2. Household appliances, Electric--Collectors and collecting--United States--Catalogs. I. Title.
TX 656.G64 1996
683'.82'075--dc20   96-22970
                                                                      CIP

Published by Schiffer Publishing, Ltd.
77 Lower Valley Road
Atglen, PA 19310
Phone: (610) 593-1777
Fax: (610) 593-2002
Please write for a free catalog.
This book may be purchased from the publisher.
Please include $2.95 for shipping.
Try your bookstore first.

We are interested in hearing from authors
with book ideas on related subjects.

Contents

Acknowledgments

I would like to thank:

Jim Sutherland, for his unwavering support and abundant patience.

John Lucia, Portland, OR, for networking and support.

John Dooley, head repairman at Appliance Repair Central, Portland, OR, for his help and information on appliance repair.

Chuck & Bonnie Meyer, Bellingham, WA, for all their help and support in the photographic field.

Guy Bennett of the US Postal Service for information on zip codes.

LaRhetta Gale for cleaning and style assistance.

Rand Owen for research assistance.

Mary at the St. Vincent DePaul, Portland, OR.

David Wiener of Appliance Rebirthing, Hartford, CT, for invaluable information.

Charlie Rook, historian at Westinghouse, for information on the company's history

Frank Friday of General Electric, for his valuable information on the company's history.

Sharon Hussing of Sunbeam Oster Corporation, for sending information on Sunbeam and the article on Ivar Jepson

Kathy Melcher of the Rival Corp. for sending a history of the company

Cindy Vogel's office at Mirro Corp. for supplying history of the company

Bernie Kiefer at West Bend Co. for supplying extensive literature on West Bend.

Introduction

In the almost fifteen years since the first books on "electric collectibles" appeared, the interest in this field has slowly but undeniably grown. Appliance collectors, Deco devotees, and industrial design fanatics are converging onto a new and enjoyable area of collecting. The early electric kitchen appliances from the 'teens and 1920s have constituted a popular collecting field for years. Many kitchen appliances from the 1940s and later have been attracting attention as well. In 1995, *U.S. News & World Report* observed the following in their Top 10 antique and collectible categories to watch for: "Appliances and other household devices—Toasters, waffle irons, electric fans and even manual typewriters from the 1940s and 1950s are sparking interest. A turquoise enamel 1950s vintage toaster may bring $125, a chrome and Bakelite 1940s toaster $40-$60."

There are many great reasons to start exploring the field of vintage appliances: they have enormous nostalgic appeal ("We had one of those!"), they were beautifully designed, and were generally built to last a lifetime. And, also important, they can be found relatively easily. For many collectors, having a vintage toaster or waffle iron in gleaming chrome with streamlined or aerodynamic styling is like owning a miniature sculpture. If you grew up with a beautiful chrome and Bakelite kitchen appliance, nostalgia is your ticket. If you are too young to have remembered them, this is an affordable and practical piece of the recent past that's relatively attainable now. Whether you just want one old appliance to use and admire or if you want to fill your room with electric percolators—this book is for you! It provides descrip-

tions of different types of metal and their applications, a discussion of the evolution of the appliance industry, and historical backgrounds on the companies and manufacturers. Featured will be examples of many of the appliances to be found in the collecting field. The book concludes with a side-trip through the world of metal kitchenware, from canisters to cooky presses, dustpans to juicers, with a section on collectible pots and pans from the 1940s and later.

I hope this book will encourage more interest in vintage appliances and kitchenware. Any piece rescued from a junk shop or yard sale, cleaned up to running or useable condition, is another useful and beautiful contribution.

Please read this section carefully! The prices in this book are based upon the following factors: comparative price listings, prices observed at shops and sales, and availability and condition. If they seem on the high side remember this: **THE PRICES LISTED IN THIS BOOK ARE FOR PIECES IN EXCELLENT CONDITION.** Needless to say, the appliance *must* be working to get a decent price. Some electric appliances have multiple parts—all these parts *must* be together to ask a higher price. Kitchenware, mainly those made of steel such as utensils, are easily subject to corrosion, which can affect pricing. The price ranges in this book are meant to accommodate the variance of prices nationwide, including urban and rural areas. Ultimately, the final price you pay is between you and the seller.

Advertisement for coffee-maker by Wear Ever, from *Good Housekeeping,* October 1954.

Chapter 1
The Electric Age

Edison Came to Stay

In the pre-electric world, power was usually supplied by animals, water mills, or steam. For lighting, the major source of energy was gas. Then came electricity.

The first main sources of electrical power were electrical batteries. These had been developed in the late eighteenth and early nineteenth centuries by such men as Luigi Galvani, Michael Faraday, and Alessandro Volta. By the mid-1800s, less than 1% of homes had electricity, in the form of door bells, call bells, and annunciators, all run by electrical batteries. The electrical current these batteries gave off is called DC ("Direct Current"), since it travels directly from source to object.

Electrical Contrivances for the Home

❦ Where **ELECTRICITY** is used in the home for **LIGHTING**, there are numerous little convenient appliances which may be attached to any lighting circuit or fixture, and which more than double the value of our service to the family. With an **ELECTRIC CHAFING DISH** you can be independent of the kitchen range any time of the day or night. The cost of operation is trifling.

❦ You are cordially invited to visit our **WAREROOMS AT 147-149 SEVENTH STREET.** The display of electrical cooking and heating devices **for the household will interest you.**

❦ **REDUCED RATES** for current on meter basis. Call Main 6688 for information.

Portland Railway Light & Power Co.

Advertisement promoting the use of electricity for purposes other than lighting, circa 1906.

But it wasn't enough to prove the theory of electricity through door bells. A better use had to be made of electricity's vast potential.

By 1876, Thomas A. Edison had begun developing an electric light with a crew of scientists and helpers at his Menlo Park, New Jersey, laboratory. In 1878, financier J. P. Morgan and others formed the Edison Electric Light Company to help continue financing Edison's experiments. Finally, in 1879, Edison successfully passed an electrical current through a carbonized filament, creating the first practical incandescent light on Direct Current (DC).

Edison used his Menlo Park farm as a sample home for electric lighting. He wired the house, workers' dormitories, laboratory, and even the barn with indoor lights. The outside also had electric lamps. When J.P. Morgan and the other backers saw this display, they were overwhelmed. So impressed were they that in 1882, Edison Electric opened Pearl Street Station, the first commercial lighting plant, in New York City. It was no coincidence that Pearl Street was located in the midst of the palatial homes of the wealthy (including J.P. Morgan). This lighting was on direct current power and by its very nature could travel only a few blocks.

Still, it was a start. Soon, Edison Electric expanded. Many small electrical transmission firms started to spring up.

Competition from Westinghouse

In 1886, George Westinghouse formed the Westinghouse Electric Company. He was advocating a new kind of current that would revolutionize the future of electricity—and also spark a bitter feud with Edison. Westinghouse's current was called Alternate Current (AC). It had been developed for Westinghouse by Nicola Tesla in the form of a horsepower motor. Alternate current was much more powerful than direct current, and it could travel for miles, instead of just a few blocks. Interest in AC power was immediate.

However, Edison remained convinced that DC power was superior to AC, placing him in direct opposition to Westinghouse. As Westinghouse got more aggressive in his promotion and sales, Edison let his feelings be known. Soon, both men had mounted campaigns to discredit the others. Around 1889, a consultant for Edison "strongly sponsored the legal adoption of AC power for state electrocution and recommended the purchase of Westinghouse alternators for the purpose."[1] Once AC power was accepted for electrocution, "Edison attacked the use of AC power by intensive propaganda on a national scale,"[2] playing heavily on its dangerous power and its grim association with death.

But Edison's smear campaign did not work. Gradually, people came to see Westinghouse's AC power as less threatening, and it became more popular. Its attributes won out, especially the fact that it could be produced "many miles from the consumer, transmitted through high tension wires, and delivered to the customer both efficiently and cheaper than DC power."[3]

The truth of the matter is that Edison, for once, was wrong. Edison's backers did not support his views any more than the public did, and in 1889 the Edison Electric Light Company was reorganized as the Edison General Electric Company. In 1892, the company merged with the Thomson-Houston Electric Company to form the General Electric Company. Thomas-Houston's president, Charles Coffin, became president of the new consolidated firm. Thomas Edison was slowly shuffled to the back.

THE GROWTH OF THE ELECTRIC INDUSTRY

Edison's light and Westinghouse's motor were the beginnings of a new age. Around 1900, the first year that electricians were classified as a separate "gainful occupation," there were over ten thousand lighting plants (now called power stations) in the United States.

At this time, too, power stations had not yet realized that promoting and selling electrical appliances would encourage the use of their current. They were primarily concerned with the promotion of electric lighting over gaslight. When appliance salesmen first tried to persuade power companies to sell the new current-consuming devices, most were totally uninterested. Some appliances were sold in hardware and department stores, but they were still a rarity.

This disregard would change, though. Many stores began to carry limited numbers of appliances, and public fascination grew. Wanamaker's department store in New York became the first major store to embrace the electric appliance field, staging an exposition called "Electro-Domestic Science" in 1906. Produced by the New York Electrical Society, the exposition featured a model electric kitchen and bedroom to show how extensively electricity could be used.

Advertisement for a tabletop electric grill by General Electric, from *Sunset Magazine*, October 1912. The small copy near the top reads "Dainty meals cooked on glowing coils."

Advertisement for General Electric, stating that although the cost of living was exploding in the Roaring Twenties, the cost of electricity was standing still, from *Redbook Magazine*, June 1926.

When power companies finally realized their own potential, they wasted no time in jumping into the appliance fray. They started manufacturing their own appliances and enlisted the help of retail businesses to place their appliances before the public. "The small kitchen appliance field was America's most active growth industry during 1890-1930."[4]

By the 1920s, electricity had been completely accepted as an indispensable servant of humankind.

However, many urban areas had outdated (DC) or substandard power, and much of rural America had not yet been electrified. The Rural Electrification Administration, a part of the New Deal, helped bring electricity to many rural areas. By World War II the United States had generally accepted a 60 cycle, 110 volt alternating current as an electrical generation standard.

THE WAR YEARS:
TANKS, NOT TOASTERS

A WAR BRIDE EQUIPS HER KITCHEN

"'What am I going to do about things for my kitchen?' is the current cry of many brides. Marie was in a quandary too! She didn't expect to stock her kitchen with all the pre-war conveniences, but she did need the essentials for keeping house. A trip to the housewares department, however, proved surprising—glass, pottery, wood, and limited supplies of plastic had stepped into the shoes of many old favorites in new variations. To be sure, choices were limited, but necessities were available.

"If you are equiping a new kitchen or replacing worn-out utensils, remember that we are at war! The boys are getting along without home cooking and soft beds and we too must eliminate frills. We all know that the high American standard has taken a temporary slump. Basic equipment is still permitted—the rest has gone into combat.

"The following list is planned for the bride just starting out. Manufacture of the above items is permitted, but this does not guarantee full stocks in all stores. On the other hand, some leftover pre-war utensils not included in this list may be found.

"KITCHEN EQUIPMENT GUIDE -
Minimum List in Today's Materials

1	large knife (metal)
1	paring knife (metal)
1	kitchen fork (metal)
1	set measuring spoons (plastic)
2	medium size spoons (plastic)
1	mixing spoon (wood)
1	rotary beater (metal)
1	can opener (metal)
1	potato masher (wood)
1	strainer (plastic, metal)
1	grater (plastic)
1	fruit juicer (plastic, glass)
1	rolling pin (wood)
1	set measuring cups (plastic)
1	measuring cup (glass)
1	spatula (metal)

1	set mixing bowls (glass, pottery)
1	covered saucepan (glass, pottery)
1	skillet (glass, metal)
1	double boiler (glass, enameledware)
1	covered casserole (glass, pottery)
1	piepan (glass, pottery)
1	square cake pan (glass)
1	coffeepot (glass, enameledware)
	Mops (usual materials)
	Dustpan and brush (no metal)
	Broom (no metal)
	Garbage pail (galvanized metal)
	Carpet sweeper (wood and metal)
	Dishpan (enameledware)
	Ironing Boards (no metal)
	Scouring pads (treated fibers)

— *From a Ladies Home Journal, February 1944 article by Florence Kas & Betty Tompkins*

Despite all the advances made to bring electricity to everyone and the proliferation of electric appliances on the market, World War II brought consumer development to a halt. The conversion to a wartime economy and the manufacture of wartime products, together with limitations set by the War Production Board and price-setting by the Office of Price Administration, caused most appliances to virtually disappear. By 1942, manufacturers had ceased production of many major goods, including electric appliances. Steel was going for tanks, not toasters.

Only in rare cases did the War Production Board grant allotments of material for non-war production. For example, in 1944 twenty manufacturers were permitted to make two million irons, particularly the traveling irons which were necessary in wartime.

Much of the morale of the Second World war homefront was kept bolstered by the promise of tomorrow. Like a child who is told if he cleans his room he can have an ice cream cone later, Americans were kept focused on war work and doing with what they had by being promised what they would have when the war was won (by them, of course). Backed by their use in wartime and their vast potential, modern technologies like electronics, optics, sonics, and atomic energy seemed relatively easy to convert to household use to "ease the load" of the housewife and family, particularly the ones who had waited so long. Periodicals, magazines and trade journals were filled with articles extolling the promises of such technologies. Many of these "inventions" have never materialized, while some, predicted back then as "just around the corner", have become popular only recently. A classic example is "Your Home Tomorrow" from the Woman's Home Companion July 1943 by J.D. Ratcliff. Maybe it would be best just to give you a sampling of the author's predictions, based on his talks with scientists, researchers and industrial executives: " The electric goods industry will make war-born servants your peacetime servants. Take the camera and picture tubes used on the war front. . . How many trips do you make upstairs to the nursery each night to see if the baby is covered? Wouldn't it be easier. . .to flick a switch on a small viewing screen. . .to see what was happening in the nursery? Television will also arrive. . .The images on your television screen will be in color and probably three-dimensional. . .Even the telephone is in for improvements. You are out. The phone rings and an electronic voice answers for you. . .If your caller leaves a message, it is recorded on a strip of metal. . .which you play back when you come home. The message can be rubbed out electrically and ready to use again. . .You have probably heard of military walkie-talkies. . .tomorrow they will move into civilian life. Suppose the baby is sick. . .the nurse in his office tells you he is out but he is carrying a small walkie-talkie.She will relay your message to him and he can get to your sick child promptly. . .Low-cost electric eyes will open doors for you. . .Electric water heaters will switch on while you sleep and electric coffee makers will start the coffee when your alarm goes off." The Author finally hints at the useful possibilities of Uranium 235: "A four ounce chunk of this stuff may heat your home for thirty years or run your car for a lifetime!!"

Appliance dealers were the hardest hit by this conversion. They had to "make do" selling appliances that already existed. Needless to say, the appliance repair industry flourished. Some dealers rescued appliances from scrap piles and repaired them, slapped "for the duration of the war" stickers on them, and sold them for $2 to $5. Even the War Production Board mounted a campaign to have consumers sell spare small electric appliances to dealers for reconditioning and resale. Scrap metal drives made matters worse—many old irons, toasters, and other appliances which might have been repaired were collected and melted down. To stay in business, some dealers launched into patriotic campaigns like "swap your old appliances for war stamps." Others diversified into non-electric items.

For consumers, too, the war years were about "making do with what you have." In 1943, *Good Housekeeping* proclaimed, "You Can Make Your Electric Equipment Last Till Victory"! The Appliance Lady told "The Tale of the Waffle Wizard" in *Woman's Home Companion* in February 1942: "He made wonderful waffles—the whole gang said so—but he didn't bother to clean up the baker when he was through and next time it was used the leftover grease and batter had baked on, especially 'round the hinge. Then, too late, conscience goaded him into trying to clean it and he had to scrub so hard he injured the chrome finish—and incurred the wrath of the Lady Wizard." Housewives were also warned in a 1945 issue of *Good Housekeeping* that cord care was just as important as the appliance, because cords were hard to get.

In an effort to fill the gap left by the requisitioning of metals, many consumers turned to wood, glass, pottery, and plastics. Plastic kitchen utensils, wooden bread boxes, glass and ceramic bakeware and cookware, and scouring pads made of cotton-wrapped scrap wire were some of the popular alternatives during the war years.

By 1944, Allied victories seemed to insure that the war's end was approaching. Still, the appliance industry had no idea what the future would hold, and when they would be able to resume production. Manufacturers had considerable differences of opinion about how soon volume production of household appliances would begin. Some predicted that production would not start for at least six months after the surrender of Germany and Japan. But things were changing: by 1945 the War Production Board was slowly granting allotments to manufacturers, primarily for major appliances like refrigerators. Consumers were cautioned that the first refrigerators off the lines would be very close cousins to the last ones.

THE POST-WAR PERIOD

With the end of the war in 1945, the Office of Price Administration lifted the barriers to production of all electric appliances. "Your days of patient waiting are over," said Marcia Knight in the January 1946 issue of *House Beautiful*, "for old electrical friends, and new, are trickling on to shop counters. There won't be many at first, but keep your fingers crossed, and you may find a returnee on your kitchen shelves."

When it came to allotments, smaller kitchen appliances got the short end of the stick. Because most steel and new technology were allotted to larger appliances (particularly refrigerators) and because there was so much red tape, the electric appliance industry lagged. At the same time, sales and promotion campaigns had whetted the buying public's appetite with promises and store window displays of appliances to come. Consumers assumed that articles advertised, listed, or shown in a dealer's salesroom were actually available—but this was often not the case. These items were displayed for the purpose of "sales potential." As a salesman of the day might have said, "They're produced primarily to give the dealer something to talk about and the customer something to look at."

Consumers Research Bulletin predicted that normal production of electrical appliances might not begin until the end of 1946, and that post-war appliances would be the same models that had been available just before the factories converted to war production in the spring of 1942. Even worse, a huge postwar steel strike in 1946/47 slowed production to a near-halt.

By the time the first shipments rolled in to retail stores around the beginning of 1947, the pent up demand for goods was so great it overwhelmed retailers. The public was tired of hearing stories of a distant future filled with electronic kitchens; they wanted their simple, reliable models back—and they wanted them now!

Fortunate housewives who reached stores when the first shipments arrived could take home a new washer or iron, among other necessities. But the chance for a new toaster was slim. Much of the steel that used to make small appliances went to larger, more urgently needed items like washers. Toast for breakfast each morning is great, but it is more important to have clean clothes all the time!

As the market improved for large appliances over the next few years, small appliances began to return in earnest. But each appliance see-sawed in production availability: coffee makers were down 57% of 1948's unit shipments, hotplates 38%, and irons 25%; on the other hand, waffles irons gained 70% and toasters 45%. (Televisions, by the way, did a 385% gain that year!) But by the end of 1949, there was a sharp sales upturn. Even small appliances were doing well. With more money to spend, consumers were shopping and the dealers were offering lower prices and easy credit (as little as $5 down would put a washing machine or a freezer in your home).

Though the Korean War in the early 1950s held back some production and materials, the boom continued. Each year, the appliance industry predicted that the next would be the best. The population explosion known as the baby boom created a unprecedented demand for electric appliances.

By 1952, though, the market had been saturated. Toasters had passed their peak, with other small appliances close behind. Housewives had acquired all the basic equipment they needed. The appliance

Advertisement showing various GE appliances, from the *Portland Shopping News,* October 1950.

industry turned to three methods to save its neck: the first was to phase out all old lines and models; the second to upgrade, redesign, and stress new models and new lines; and the third was to increase sales pressure. It seems to have worked; 1955 became the best year ever for appliances. New appliances, introduced in crude forms after the war, became available to consumers in sleeker 1950s styling with technical improvements—televisions (of course), air conditioners, home freezers, hair dryers, and the new electric frypan, which premiered in 1954.

A nice sunny kitchen with electric appliances and kitchenware, from *Ladies Home Journal,* February 1957.

IT'S THERMOSTATIC!

"Only four years ago none of us had heard of skillets, sauce pans, double boilers or deep fryers with precise built in heat control. But in those four years this new family of small appliances has been so widely bought and so much liked they have begun to affect the rest of the kitchen. Since these appliances are entirely portable, you can cook all over the kitchen. As a result, you need plenty of outlets and plenty of wattage. And the number of "burners" you need is greatly reduced. Born of all this are two new products: the "Plug-in Strip" which runs along the back of the counter and provides an electrical outlet every 18 inches and the "plug-in center," with 3 retractable cords, two outlets and automatic timing units supplying electricity for 5 appliances."

—*excerpted from an article in House Beautiful June 1957 entitled "How the Thermostatic Appliance has changed the Kitchen"*

The biggest boost for the appliance trade came in 1956. In that year, General Electric was joined by over seventy utilities nationwide to usher in the nationwide "Living Better Electrically" campaign. Just as their predecessors had learned during the early days of electricity, they knew that selling "Electric Living" was also selling electric goods. An official from GE summed it up: "The industry is out to increase its fair share of the consumers disposable dollars. Population and employment are on the upswing and housing is holding up. We don't see why cars should run away with all the money!" The campaign distrib-

uted a short movie to be shown in movie theaters and produced an hour-long TV show for consumers. Simultaneously, the Edison Electric Company initiated its own national drive, called Operation House Power. While these campaigns did sell more appliances for the companies' profit, they also educated consumers, who became more likely to ask about wiring, wattage, and brand names than they had in the past.

The advances and economics of the appliance field continued on an even course into the 1960s and beyond. All-electric kitchens became more common, and the nickel-cadmium battery unleashed a plethora of cordless appliances. The fitness craze and the gourmet and international food craze, not to mention the health food revolution that began in the 1970s, has introduced into our modern kitchens many electric appliances a 1940s housewife would find amazing: bread makers, pasta machines, microwaves, yogurt makers, food processors, and espresso machines. She would recognize the old stand-bys—toasters, blenders, etc.—but might find their minimal designs and all-plastic bodies amusing.

INDUSTRIAL DESIGN

Undeniably, industrial design has become one of the fastest-growing areas of collectibles from the 1920s-1960s era. What was just a mere glimmer ten years ago has become a fascinating and challenging field of collecting. "Industrial design" is just that—the design of any object that was in some way industrially manufactured. This includes electric appliances, furniture, vacuum cleaners, tools, microphones, cameras, telephones, serving pieces, and much more. At one time, being designed by a famous (or relatively well-known) industrial designer was a major selling point.

In the 1920s and 1930s, manufacturers turned to industrial designers for solutions. The population was increasing, accompanied by a major increase in advertising and publications aimed at women and homeowners. There was growing demand for quantities of goods that could be mass-produced yet still well-designed and appealing. Technology was changing as well, and new products (like electric appliances) needed newer, modern designs. Materials were available that had previously not been fully utilized: processed aluminum, chrome, plastics, and stainless steel. These influences forced the manufacturers to update their designs and production.

The work of industrial designers is closely linked with the Art Deco movement in America. Indeed, the industrial designers played a major role in the style's evolution. Industrial designers were influenced by machines, factories, science, science fiction, and large modes of transportation—cars, planes, trains, and ships. Many designers, who had actually helped design these machines, applied the "streamlined" look on a smaller scale, to lamps, chairs and other home furnishings. This was copied in other design fields such as the decorative arts, jewelry, and posters, proliferating just about everywhere.

Industrial designers, however, delved further into utilitarian design, working with new technologies and refining designs. They designed radios, telephones, irons, clocks, appliances, fans, and countless other products. This continued through the 1940s, when the military made use of the designers' talents for their own industrial needs.

After the war, the hey-day of the industrial designer was far from over. Many of the most celebrated designers of the pre-war era were still active. They contributed to redesigning objects for a post-war nation. Though their names weren't as prominently displayed, they were busy designing our refrigerators, ranges, lawn mowers, dinnerware sets, school furniture, motorboats, mixing bowls, scissors, and spatulas. One designer, once famous for Art Deco lamps, clocks, and the like, went on to redesign the logos and packaging for such popular post-war products Joy detergent, Prell shampoo, and Gleem toothpaste.

WHAT'S COMING FOR YOUR KITCHEN

"Gaze into a crystal ball at appliances to be for your kitchen. These designs are not available yet - but watch for them. They may be on the market within the next five years. Preview the future, here and now, with some of the following items: a 58 inch compact *Cooking center* includes electronic oven and regular oven with rotisserie, cooking top "drawer" which slides into recess when not in use, ventilators, strip lighting and a panel of push buttons which control all operations; *Ultrasonic dishwashers* which utilize inaudible, high frequency sound waves to agitate water and scrub dishes; *Microwave cooking* - eggs in 45 seconds, boil water in 2 minutes and fry bacon in little over one minute - faster than you had dreamed possible. Microwave tube that sends out "cooking" waves is directly below fiberglass disc that holds food. A panel of switches on wall will command perforated hood to drop down and cover disc. Hood automatically goes up when timer rings; *Radio-controlled oven*. By pressing a button a radio transmitter, you'll be able to turn oven in kitchen on, or off, or change the temperature though 25 miles away on a gadget small enough to fit into your pocket or purse. Wonderful when shopping or visiting. Nice, too, if you want to have dinner going while you're in church, or off on an errand somewhere."

—excerpted from an article in Better Homes and Garden September 1958 entitled "What's Coming for your Kitchen"

The legacy of the industrial designers is a two-edged sword. They left us with a vast amount of incredibly beautiful (and collectible) objects which served their purposes well and have stood the test of time. In the America of today, though, the industrial designer would be of little use. Concurrently, in a product-conscious and over-polluted world, an industrial designer could be considered a damnable co-conspirator, rather than a bringer of beauty and convenience.

All this conjecture shouldn't keep you from the field of industrial design as collectible. Mostly anything from before World War II is desirable, from jukeboxes to cigarette boxes. A group of industrial designers in the 1920s and 1930s is associated with designing serving and utilitarian pieces in chrome and aluminum, the "now" materials of the day. These objects are usually described as "high style Deco." Art Deco, chrome and industrial design collectors have already acquired much of what's available in this field. Still, items from this genre turn up frequently, though usually just a single piece or two at a time—sets are rare. Look for tea sets, coffee sets, serving bowls, beer sets, smoking accessories, platters, trays, thermoses, flatware, and utensils. Often the metal is used with wood, bamboo, raffia, or some of the popular plastics—Catalin, Bakelite, or Urea. There were many "knock-offs" of designs by famous designers from that time period.

Post-war items include numerous kitchen and household appliances, as well as utilitarian objects for offices, schools and other institutions. Postwar designers didn't always get their names promoted with the item, as they had in pre-war times, so it might be hard to identify some of these pieces.

A major problem with collecting objects from the industrial design era is their lack of availability now. While many of these objects were mass-produced in the hundreds of thousands, they can nonetheless be scarce. Tony Fusco sums up the reason very nicely in his 1988 book on Art Deco:

When something nice by Grandmother went out of fashion—a vase, a Chanel dress, a Tiffany lamp, a table, a chrome coffee service—she wasn't likely to throw it away. It was packed away in the attic or given to a child who was setting up his or her own apartment. The situation was very different with industrial design. When a pressing iron had outlived its usefulness it was not enshrined with the family photos; it was thrown out on the junk heap. Even broken vases can be glued. Broken pencil sharpeners are just replaced.

As you research industrial design, you are sure to see the work of Russel Wright, Raymond Loewy, Paul Frankl, Donald Deskey, Walter Dorwin Teague, Norman Bel Geddes, and Henry Dreyfus.

[1] Fredgant, Don. *Electric Collectibles*. Padre Productions, San Luis Obispo, CA.
[2] Ibid.
[3] Ibid.
[4] Ibid.

Advertisement from the American Gas Association pushing the virtues of gas appliances, from *Better Homes & Gardens*, December 1953

CHAPTER 2
Types of Metal

Here is a quick look at the metals used for electric appliances, cookware, and kitchenware in the twentieth century. We really are talking about just five metals—some new, some old. Remember, they are not all the same: every shiny metal isn't chrome, nor does aluminum come in just one finish. Learning to recognize the nature of these metals will make your collecting easier.

ALUMINUM
Chemical Symbol Al

Aluminum is a lightweight, silver-colored metal that can be formed into almost any shape. Pure aluminum is soft and has little strength. Therefore it is usually alloyed with other elements to create one of our most versatile metals. The world uses more aluminum than any other metal except iron and steel. Aluminum is also the most plentiful metallic element in the earth's crust, making up 8%. Until the mid-1800s, aluminum was more expensive than gold and silver, but when scientists learned how to refine bauxite to get aluminum, the price of aluminum dropped from $115 a pound to $17 a pound. By 1910 The Aluminum Company of America (ALCOA) was producing aluminum for 30¢ a pound!

Aluminum production soared during World War I as the fighting nations increased output to fill their needs. This was helped by the development of an inexpensive smelting process around 1914. The 1920s and 1930s saw improved methods of turning aluminum into useful household and kitchen products. Aluminum was not so quickly embraced as a fine metal as chrome or copper had been. Its dull finish did not mimic silver's richness and its light weight felt cheap and industrial. When the designer Russel Wright introduced a line of serving pieces in aluminum in the 1930s, people were aghast.

ALL-OUT WAR IN TIN CAN ALLEY

"In the 1950s, the aluminum companies, particularly Reynolds Aluminum Co., were trying to make a dent into the steel company-dominated tin can business. Aluminum companies for years had been foraging for new outlets for their products, Faced with overcapacity, they badly needed a major market on a commodity basis. To get into these markets meant displacing steel.

"When Reynolds Co. first approached the can companies in the early 1950s, the meeting had been less than productive. The can companies were put off by Reynolds over zealous self-promotion and a paternal-like desire to protect their relationship with steel. Seeing no result over the years, Reynolds felt that the canmakers were freezing aluminum out. The aluminum companies had been looking for a can in which steel held the least competitive advantage. It was decided the 6 oz. frozen orange juice can would be the best because it didn't have to be particularly strong and its corrosive resistance was a valuable asset, as was its light weight for shipping purposes, since the packing is handles close to the fruit source.

"In January, 1960 Reynolds went into action. They put a can line from its packaging lab in Richmond, Virginia on a truck trailer and drove it down to the Minute Maid Corp. plant in Florida City. There, backed up to the receiving dock, the can line turned out 7 million cans in 3 weeks. Minute Maid liked the idea so much it leased the can line and installed it permanently. Birds Eye Foods followed suit, as did other packers. The in-plant can line gave packers a powerful club over the canmakers, who had no choice but to make their product more competitive. In late 1960, the steel industry announced a new double-reduced thin tinplate for canmaking. This, of course, upped the ante and triggered a fierce price war. By late 1961, both sides were head to head, with the canning companies using 50% aluminum and 50% tinplate. With a comfortable niche established, Reynolds turned its sight to the beer can industry . . . but that's another story."

— *Excerpted from an article in Business Week magazine, November 1961*

During World War II, aluminum was sent off to the "front line" of production, to be used for military materials. After the war, aluminum became all-important, slowly replacing other metals in the kitchen and elsewhere. During the early 1950s, the Korean war gobbled up much of the aluminum supply, forcing housewives to guard their aluminum pots and pans jealously. Today, aluminum kitchen and household item from the 1950s are becoming just as desirable. Aluminum foil and beverage cans are two products of the post-war world that are commonplace today.

Care and Cleaning: For all of aluminum's admirable traits, it has some unfortunate drawbacks, too. Aluminum utensils and cookware discolor easily and can discolor "certain foods" it comes in contact with as well. (**Note**: When you hear that "certain foods" will cause damage to metalware, they are talking about ACIDIC foods and substances. These include tomatoes, vinegar, salt, alcohol, and any products made with these. Softer metals like iron, copper, and aluminum are more susceptible. High mineral contents in tap water will cause damage as well. This piece of information applies to all metals henceforth discussed.) Discoloring can be corrected by boiling utensils or pots in an acid solution of two tablespoons of cream of tartar to one quart of water for 5 to 10 minutes. Do not clean aluminum with harsh soaps or abrasives. There are aluminum cleaners on the market (I use a Comet-like powder called Cameo). Read the labels and DO NOT use a product that says "Do not use on Aluminum". Believe me, they know what they are talking about! Aluminum also tarnishes, forming a dull gray film that is not always noticeable but is easily removed by a simple cleaning. Aluminum pits easily no matter how high the quality of product purchased. This pitting can mar the appearance of the product and is not reversible once it starts. Constant cleaning is the best preventative measure.

CHROMIUM (CHROME)
Chemical Symbol Cr

Chromium is a chemical element that is a glossy, gray metal. Better known as chrome, it is highly rust resistant and becomes bright and shiny when pol-

Advertisement for Everedy chrome products, from *Better Homes & Gardens*, December 1953.

Advertisement for Wear Ever aluminum products, from *Better Homes & Gardens*, October 1952.

ished. For these reasons, chrome is widely used to plate other metals, giving them a durable, shiny finish. Chrome hardens steel and is commonly combined with steel to produce stainless steels. Chrome is also mixed with other elements to form color compounds. The word chromium comes form the Greek word *chroma* meaning color.

In nature, chromium is almost always found combined with iron and oxygen in a mineral called chromite. A French chemist, Louis Vauquekin, prepared the first free chromium metal in 1780. But chrome sat at the starting gate until World War I when chromium plating techniques (thanks to electricity) were perfected and put to war use. In the 1920s, chrome joined two other popular metals, copper and brass, in use on household and decorative furnishings. During the Depression, people could not afford silver. Chrome, brass and copper were solutions for filling the gap, particularly chrome, which gave the illusion of fine silver. At this same time, chrome replaced nickel as the major plating material on appliances. Chrome's popularity would increase until World War II, when it became allotted to war use. After the war, stainless steels and aluminum would start to push chrome to the back of the line.

Care and Cleaning: Chrome is beautiful, but not indestructible. Although it is rust resistant, excessive exposure to harsh chemicals or water will cause less expensive chrome plating to deteriorate, thus exposing the metal underneath (usually steel). Do NOT use harsh abrasive cleansers or rough steel wool on chrome—it scratches easily. Mild soap and water and a soft drying cloth will keep chrome objects bright and shiny. Brasso also works well when you get on one of those polishing jags.

NICKEL
Chemical Symbol Ni

Nickel is a white metallic element usually found alloyed with other elements or metals. Pure nickel was first isolated in 1751. Nickel takes a high polish resembling silver, but does not tarnish. Nickel is also resistant to rust. Because of these qualities, nickel was used extensively for electroplating in the first part of the twentieth century. "Nickel-plated" appliances were made up to the 1930s, when chrome became the preferred metal for plating objects. The largest use of nickel today is as an additive to cast iron and steel, making them resistant to corrosion and impact. "Armor-plated" objects are often nickel/steel alloys. We also have nickel to thank for the nickel-cadmium battery, which is "rechargeable" and lasts much longer than standard batteries.

Mention should be made of another nickel alloy called **Nickel silver**. It is a yellowish metal alloy of nickel, copper, and zinc. Nickel silver tarnishes easily but takes a high polish. Much of the silverware used today is made of nickel silver plated with real silver. It looks like solid silver when new, but the plate can wear off with age. I'm not aware if nickel silver was used in flatware or cooking utensils in the past decades—but it could have been.

Care and Cleaning: You won't encounter many nickel plated objects in your appliance and kitchenware collecting, unless you are collecting pre-1930s. Since nickel is so similar to chrome, see the previous cleaning directions for chrome. Nickel silver, as mentioned, is found mostly as the base for flatware. Be wary of using any older flatware where the silver plate has worn off. Ingestion of nickel silver has been known to make people sick.

COPPER
Chemical symbol Cu

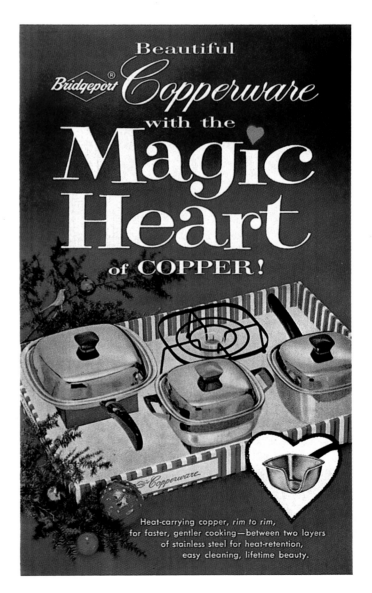

Advertisement for copper-cored and copper-clad cookware by Bridgeport Brass Co., from *Better Homes & Gardens*, December 1956.

Copper is a rich orange in color, but when exposed to the weather, it assumes its characteristic greenish patina. Copper was one of the first metals to be discovered by man. Because it is a superb conductor of heat, copper has been used in the United States for cookware since colonial times. Copper-clad cookware (that is, cookware with a copper-coated bottom) is common in modern times as well.

Copper is also one of the best low-cost conductors of electricity. By the late 1800s, the rapid growth of electric lighting and telephone systems had greatly increased the demand for copper, which dwindling deposits of high grade ore could not meet. Fortunately (and in the nick of time), in 1900, an American mining engineer developed a way to extract copper from low-grade ore. This increased copper production ten-fold. Copper's utilitarian and aesthetic qualities were re-embraced by the Arts and Crafts Movement at the beginning of the twentieth century.

Two familiar copper alloys are **Bronze** and **Brass**. **Bronze** is an alloy of copper and tin. It is harder and more durable then copper and assumes a similar patina. It is still used for casting statues, medals, and bells. **Brass** is a cheaper substitute for bronze, being alloyed of zinc and copper. It has a golden shine and polishes well. This makes it very desirable for decorative objects. In fact, brass was extremely popular at the beginning of the twentieth century, as chrome and stainless steel would become later on. Brass automobile fixtures, chandeliers, and bed frames were common.

Care and Cleaning: Copper is used in cookware for its quick, even heat distribution. Never cook in solid copper pots as its combination with "certain foods" (primarily acidic) can be poisonous. Copper serving pieces are safe, since the food is not being cooked in them. To clean discolored copper, spray a cloth with a vinegar and salt solution, rub the copper, and rinse it in hot water—or use Brasso and a soft cloth.

Stainless Steel

Stainless steel, a twentieth century wonder, is steel to which other metal alloys have been added. This combination produces a steel that has an easily maintained, attractive appearance with remarkable strength and high resistance to corrosion. Most stainless steels used in the home are highly polished with an attractive silver-like appearance. Look for stainless steel on electrical appliances (old and new), knives, utensils, and most importantly, pots and pans.

Chromium (Chrome) is the chief metal alloyed with steel to make stainless steel tough and rust resistant. Only alloys of steel that contain at least 10% Chromium are called stainless steel. Nickel ranks as the second most important alloy in making stainless steel. Chrome-plated and stainless steel objects are so similar in appearance that they are hard to distinguish.

Care and Cleaning: Stainless steel cookware's poor heat conductivity is offset by plating it over aluminum or copper, or by coating the bottom with one of these two metals (known as "clad"). Stainless steel is the easiest kitchen metal to clean. Soaps, detergents, and most cleaners are safe, and stainless can take scrubbing, too. Those "certain foods," however, can cause deterioration over time. It would be wise to test any new stainless steel pot or pan by gently boiling canned tomatoes or lemon juice for about thirty minutes and then allowing them to cool. If the pot or pan exhibits a considerable amount of an etching effect on its inside surfaces, this should be taken as a sign of poor quality, and the item should be promptly returned or discarded.

CHAPTER 3

The Companies

There would be nothing to collect if it wasn't for the manufacturers and companies that produced and sold appliances. Following are company-by-company histories of most of the major players in the appliance field in the period covered by this book. I have also included references and dates to the more popular items or lines the company produced. You will quickly notice some companies produced primarily electric appliances. I have also included information on companies like Mirro, Foley, and West Bend, who produced mainly kitchenware and cookware items. Many of these companies products were interwoven with the appliance companies.

BETTY CROCKER

What's Betty Crocker doing in the appliance industry? That's what many in the appliance trade wondered in 1945 when General Mills Inc. announced it was entering the small appliance field. General Mills' highly advanced mechanical divisions had been making precision equipment for the armed forces during World War II. It was decided that its well-equipped factories could produce a line of electric housewares.

Another advantage was that General Mills could enter the appliance business with a powerful equity in its famous "Betty Crocker" image, which had symbolized it products for twenty-five years. There would be a close tie-in to Betty Crocker Kitchens to provide recipes and other promotional items.

The first few items released sold well, and by 1950 the two-millionth Tru-Heat iron came off the assembly line. That same year, a General Mills toaster was added to the line and in 1953, four new appliances were added, to make a line of seven in all: food mixer, automatic fry-cooker, waffle iron, automatic coffee maker, iron, steam ironing attachment, and toasters.

Despite all this output, the Betty Crocker line had faced obstacles from the beginning. The Korean war forced government restrictions on civilian production. War work and appliances were just not compatible. When General Mills saw its ambitious project facing an unsure future, it brought its appliance venture to a halt and sold the business to the McGraw Electric Company in 1954.

Advertisement for General Mills' "Betty Crocker" line, from *Woman's Home Companion*, November 1948. Electric products would emerge from the company soon after this range-top saucepan was offered.

CASCO PRODUCTS CORPORATION

In 1949 an industrial products firm, the Casco Products Corporation, ventured into the appliance field. The first item it produced was an automatic steam and dry iron. With the success of the iron, the line was expanded to include griddles and other cookware. In 1960, the company was acquired by Standard Kollsman Industries Inc.

Shortly after that, the "Lady Casco" line of appliances appeared. "Lady Casco" was based on a full line of ten "match-mate" appliances, the chief of which was the "Chef Mate." This was a unique motor-driven power base with a series of attachments including a mixer, a blender, and others. The rest of the line consists of electric toasters, coffee pots, irons, and fry pans. The "Lady Casco" line was to be offered to selected stores on a franchise arrangement. The appliances even carried an exclusive five-year warranty backed by a Lloyd's of London insurance policy! By the end of 1961, over two thousand retailers had been franchised and sales were just taking off.

Then suddenly, in early 1962, the Kollsman management decided to bring this bold and innovative venture to an end. The "Lady Casco" program was discontinued and its former, traditional method of distribution was resumed. Valiant efforts to reestablish the former Casco image were made during the following months by introducing a toothbrush, warming trays and other items. In 1963, the entire appliance line was sold to the Hamilton Beach Division of the Scovill Manufacturing Company in Waterbury, Connecticut.

A.F. DORMEYER

Manufacturing Company There would be nothing to collect if it wasn't for the manufacturers and companies that produced and sold appliances. Following are company-by-company histories of most of the major players in the appliance field in the period covered by this book. I have also included references and dates to the more popular items or lines the company produced. You will quickly notice some companies produced primarily electric appliances. I have also included information on companies like Mirro, Foley, and West Bend, who produced mainly kitchenware and cookware items. Many of these companies products were interwoven with the appliance companies.

Artist's rendition of Dormeyer products, from a Dormeyer "meal-Mixer" manual, 1949.

Though little is known of this company, it did make considerable inroads to the appliance market when it introduced a new Dormeyer electric "Household Beater" in 1927. Developed by A. F. Dormeyer, it was originally manufactured by the MacLeod Manufacturing Company and was designed so the motor could be readily detached from the bracket holding the beater blades—the idea of simply detaching the beaters didn't come until later. In the 1930s, the company changed its name to the A. F. Dormeyer Manufacturing Company, and continued its development in the field of mixers and other appliances.

FARBERWARE

Established in 1900 as S.W. Farber Inc., this company introduced the "Farberware" line of nickel- and silver-plated giftware and serving accessories around 1910. By the 1920s and 1930s the company offered chrome cookware and serving pieces, and developed a line of coffee makers and urns under names like the "Coffee Robot." In 1938 the "Broiler Robot" was introduced as "the first broiler that could cook food at the dinner table."

Advertisement showing orchids for Farberware in honor of winning the 1951 Fashion Academy Award, from *Better Homes & Gardens*.

During World War II, Farber put most of its energies into the war effort but did produce some consumer items, including a "hot water plate" which, when filled with hot water, would keep foods warm.

After the war, Farber upgraded its factories and concentrated on developing stainless steel cookware. In 1949, they introduced their famous stainless steel, aluminum-clad Farberware cookware, the first of its kind. This was followed by the first stainless steel electric frying pan in 1954. Many other successes followed.

In 1987, Farberware was sold to British-American Hanson Industries Inc.

FOLEY

Foley's success in the cookwares industry is really the success of the Aluminum Specialty Company, which was acquired by Foley in 1980. Aluminum Specialty came to Foley with an impressive history—founded in 1909, within five years it was a multimillion dollar operation. By the 1920s, ASC was producing aluminum cookware under the trade names Very Best Quality and Alumode. All consumer lines were converted to war production in the 1940s and in the early 1950s, and ASC was recognized by the Defense Department as one of the top producers in the Korean war effort. Finally, in 1958, they introduced a new cookware line called Chiltonware. (In the same year, ASC introduced the first aluminum Christmas trees!) In 1962, two more cookware lines were added, Chilton-Clad cookware made from Duranel (aluminum-clad stainless steel) and Chilton House. Foley purchased ASC in 1980 and combined it with Mirro Corporation in 1985.

GENERAL ELECTRIC

Advertisement displaying various General Electric products, from *Better Homes & Gardens*, December 1956. Any of these items would be choice finds for the collector, especially the early Toast-R-Oven and the footed teakettle.

The General Electric Company was formed in 1892 by the merger of Thomas Edison's Edison General Electric Company and the Thomson-Houston Company By 1907, GE had marketed a full line of heating and cooking devices. In 1922 the GE appliance and merchandise department was formed. GE is mainly associated with large appliances, with "Hotpoint" as a recognizable brand name. Though the company made a myriad of electric products, your search for smaller GE appliances will be a challenge.

HAMILTON BEACH

The Hamilton Beach Manufacturing Company was founded in 1911 by L. H. Hamilton and Chester Beach. The pair had developed a "universal fractional horsepower motor" which could run on both AC and DC currents. This flexibility made it very marketable, since different areas of the country used different types of electrical current.

Advertisement showing the Hamilton Beach mixer, from *Better Homes & Gardens*, December 1953. Hamilton Beach revolutionized motor driven appliances with the early AC/DC motor. Their mixer is a classic and comes with two bowls. The juicer was sold separately.

The company's first appliance also came in 1911, with the invention of a commercial drink mixer. At the time, malted milks were popular soda fountain attractions and Hamilton Beach's mixer was quite successful.

Their first success in the home appliance field came with an electric treadle sewing machine. Soon, the company was applying its motor to all sorts of home appliances. Hamilton Beach is associated mainly with kitchen appliances. One of their earliest and biggest lines was in blenders. They offered a hand-held version as well as the standard heavy tabletop version. In 1990, Hamilton Beach/ Proctor Silex, Inc. was formed out of the merger of the two companies.

KitchenAid

In the early 1900s, the Hobart Company was the world's largest manufacturer of food equipment.

Wish your kitchen a Merry Christmas !

Advertisement displaying the KitchenAid mixer by Hobart Mfg. Co, from *Good Housekeeping,* December 1956. The KitchenAid was distinct in that it appears to have one large heart-shaped beater, instead of the traditional two on other brands.

Around 1910,The first KitchenAid product, the home mixer, was developed and produced by a subsidiary of the Hobart Company, Troy Metal Products. In 1919 the first KitchenAid hand mixer hit the market and in the 1937, customers could find KitchenAid coffee grinders, the first coffee grinders made for home use, in their grocery stores. In 1949 Hobart made its entrance in the major appliance market with a home dishwasher.

By 1986 KitchenAid had become a division of Whirlpool Corporation.

Landers, Frary, and Clark (Universal)

The company of Landers, Frary and Clark was formed in 1862 when Landers and Smith Manufacturing Company acquired the Frary and Clark Company of Meriden, Connecticut. The number of products manufactured by LF&C over the years was enormous and their scope amazing. They made noserings for bulls, along with electric ranges, kitchen scales and vacuum bottles, window hardware and ice skates, mouse traps and percolators, meat hooks and can openers, cutlery and aluminum cookware, and thousands of other products.

In the 1890s, the trade name "Universal" was adopted for the company's products. At the same time, LF&C introduced a series of quite revolutionary household products including the Universal food

chopper (1897), the Universal bread maker (1895), and most important, the Universal coffee percolator (1905), which offered a brand new method of brewing coffee below the boiling point.

UNIVERSAL *Coffeematic*
with the Flavor-Selector
The fastest, finest way to good coffee. Simply set the Flavor-Selector to the strength you prefer. Coffeematic then quickly brews to perfection, signals when ready and keeps your coffee piping hot . . . all automatically.
from $24⁹⁵
ten-cup model shown, in chrome—$29.95 in copper—$32.95

The first Universal electric appliance appeared in 1912, when a "thermo cell" electric iron was introduced. Percolators, toasters and ranges soon followed. After World War I, the company continued its efforts into electrical household products, claiming that six out of every ten homes in the country had at least one Universal product.

By the 1950s, the company was starting to show cracks. It sold off some of its divisions, including cutlery, after 85 years of operations. LF&C continued to make acquisitions such as the Dazey Corporation (maker of can openers, juicers and other items) in 1954, and the Handy-Hannah Products Corporation (maker of the "Handy-Hannah" brand of kitchenware) in 1956. Despite these and other acquisitions, LF&C could not keep pace with the competition of other corporations. One of the "granddaddies" of the kitchenware industry, Landers, Frary, and Clark was acquired in 1965 by General Electric Company's Housewares Division, along with its Universal trade name.

Manning-Bowman and Company

Incorporated in 1864, Manning-Bowman and Company originally manufacturer Britannia ware, polished tinware, and porcelain enamel. By 1872, when silver plating was replacing Britannia ware, Manning-Bowman went extensively into enamelware. The company produced porcelain enamelware bowls, pitchers, coffee pots, and tea pots. It also made a line of graniteware called "Pearl Agate Ware."

The next year, 1873, the company obtained the first of a number of patents on coffee brewing devices. In 1890, Manning Bowman introduced the coffee percolator in the form we know today. The company prospered, and soon after the turn of the century it introduced electrical household appliances.

During the 1920s and 1930s, Manning Bowman produced several items for the housewares trade. Many of these items are considered very desirable by Art Deco enthusiasts. They including mantel clocks and various chrome items such as tea sets, coffee services, serving pieces, and post-Prohibition barware. Manning Bowman's Craftware was a complete line of streamlined Art Deco pieces.

Manning Bowman continued to make appliances for the home until 1946, when it was acquired by the Bersted Manufacturing Company.

McGraw Electric

Founded in 1900 by 17-year-old Max McGraw, McGraw Electric's history is one of merger and acquisitions. Max McGraw made his first acquisition in 1912. In 1926, McGraw acquired the Bersted Manufacturing Company, makers of small appliances.

McGraw enjoyed a long on-and-off-again relationship with the Bersted company. Mr. Bersted bought back his company in 1930, but sold it back to an eager McGraw in 1948. McGraw also acquired the "Tip Toe" iron from Yale and Towne Manufacturing Company that same year. In 1957, McGraw acquired Thomas A. Edison Inc. and changed its name to McGraw Edison Company. You will find all sorts of McGraw electric appliances from the 1920s on.

Mirro

Mirro's history begins with the merger of two companies, the Aluminum Manufacturing Company and the Manitowoc Novelty Company in 1909. Within five years they had produced and sold their first cookware item, an aluminum double boiler, and received their first major contract to produce aluminum hubcaps. In 1917 the company established the MIRRO brand name for all its aluminum cookware.

Mirro's contributions to World War I include aluminum canteens, mess kits, and cooking sets. Their contribution in World War II went beyond cookware to also include airplane parts, fuel tanks, and cartridge cases. Between the wars and after, the company pro-

duced waterless cookware as well as introducing it's Mirro Pressure Pan.

So well-known was the Mirro name that when the company changed its name in 1957, it changed only slightly, to Mirro Aluminum Company, and finally to Mirro Corporation in 1977. In 1983, Mirro was purchased by Newell, a manufacturing and marketing corporation. Two years late Mirro was consolidated with the Foley Company.

Advertisement displaying various Universal products, from *Woman's Home Companion*, December 1955. Universal items were not long on style but their quality and longevity have made up for it.

The Oster Manufacturing Company

The original name of this company was The John Oster Manufacturing Company, formed in 1924 by John Oster to manufacture hair clippers. Most clippers of the day were made for grooming animals. Oster clippers, modified for human use, were an instant success with barbers, beauticians, and eman-

Advertisement displaying the "Osterizer" blender, from *Better Homes & Gardens*, December 1953. Also shown in this eye-popping ad is the Oster knife sharpener in plastic body and the portable mixer.

cipated ladies eager to "bob" their hair. He also developed small motor driven clippers as well as detachable blades.

In 1935 Oster expanded his scope, bringing out the "Oster Massage," which was adopted by hospitals and sanitariums. Through World War II, Oster made motors for artillery, radios, radar transmission, and electric clippers at a volume undreamed of before the war. After the war, Oster purchased the Stevens Electric Company which had invented the drink mixer in 1922. Oster refined it into a blender for household use, and "The Osterizer" was introduced in 1946. Two years later The Osterizer was succeeded by the "Osterett," an attractive hand-held mixer.

The Oster Company was acquired by The Sunbeam Corporation in 1960.

PRESTO

Presto appliances were originally made under the trade name "National" by the Northwest Steel and Iron Works, which was established in 1905. One of their

Advertisement showing various "Presto" pressure cookers by the National Pressure Cooker Co., from *Good Housekeeping*, January 1948.

early successes was in the field of pressure cookers. In 1939, the company changed its name to the National Pressure Cooker Company and the brand name became "Presto." Presto pressure cookers were tremendous successful through the Depression, Indeed, they have been called "the microwave of the 1930s."

Presto household canners enjoyed continued success throughout World War II, as "Victory Gardens" and canning programs proliferated across the United States. After the war, however, Presto realized the need to diversify its products. The interest in canning was waning as more housewives bought refrigerators and freezers. In 1949, Presto introduced the first vapor steam iron that could use tap water.

During the 1950s, the company changed its name to the National Presto Industries Inc. and introduced a line of appliances featuring a revolutionary removable "Control Master" heat control that was interchangable among all the appliances in the group. When this electric control was disconnected, the appliances could be submerged for washing.

Presto has continued to manufacture many small appliances and "gizmos." Some of its recent "blockbuster" products include the PrestoBurger hamburger cooker (1976), the FryBaby electric deep fryer (1976), The Salad Shooter (1988), and the TaterTwister (1990).

REVERE COPPER AND BRASS, INC.

"Revere Ware" was created by Revere Copper and Brass, Inc., a company that had formed in 1928 as the merger of six companies. In the 1930s, Revere Copper and Brass worked on developing an alternative to cast iron cookware, which was still the standard cookware in most houses. In 1939 Revere Ware Copper Clad Stainless Steel Cookware was introduced and met with a tremendous response. Demand soon outpaced production capacity.

World War II halted production completely, however. Between 1942 and 1945, Revere turned out cartridge cases, smoke bombs, and rocket cases. After the war's end, Revere turned instantly to peacetime sales of Revere Ware. The Korean War took all of the copper again, so Revere manufactured many stainless steel items such as mixing bowls, canisters, utensil racks and casseroles.

During the 1950s Revere tried different lines, some of them short-lived. Hotel Ware, heavy duty cookware for industrial use, was introduced in 1954. Copper Maid Cookware, a lighter weight version of Revere Ware with a different design, was introduced in 1957. Deluxe Revere Ware Cookware, a line with a different handle and knob than Revere Ware and lids shaped like Chines pagodas, was introduced in 1962.

The 1960s saw a sharp decline in sales of Revere Ware. This long decline did not change for the better until the early 1970s. In 1988, Revere Copper and Brass was acquired by Corning Glass Works.

Give the gift of good cooking

Good cooks know *copper* cooks best. It heats fast, evenly . . . makes cooking with Revere Ware so easy and pleasant. Now your *choice* of copper-clad stainless steel Revere Ware with the famous copper bottom . . . or copper core stainless steel Designers' Group, where copper works unseen to spread heat across the bottom and up the sides. These are wonderfully useful gifts for a lifetime of good cooking! Revere Copper and Brass Incorporated, Rome, New York.

REVERE WARE
The world's finest cooking utensils

Advertisement displaying various Revere Ware products, from *Living*, April 1961. The new "Designers Group" line pictured at the bottom of the ad would be worth searching for. . . . it has a copper core instead of a clad bottom and the design of the pans are totally different.

RIVAL

The Rival Company was organized in 1932 by H.J. Talge. The company's first product, introduced shortly after, was the Juice-O-Mat, a manual citrus juicer.

This juicer would stay in Rival's product line for many years.

In 1956, after purchasing the National Slicing Machine Company, Rival began making food slicers. The following year it introduced the first electric can opener.

Rival has gone back and forth between private and public ownership since it was purchased by Stern Bros. Investment Bank in the early 1960s. Since then Rival has acquired manufacturers of ice cream freezers, space heaters, shower massagers, and sump pumps.

Rival's name will always be associated with crock pots, since in 1970 the company acquired Naxon Utilities Corporation, a manufacturer of an appliance named the Bean Pot. This bean pot was the forerunner of the very successful Crock Pot slow cooker of the 1970s.

Advertisement showing "Can-O-Mat" by Rival, from *House & Garden*, December 1961. Can openers were still relatively new in 1961, so the ad is very accurate when it says "New for the Kitchen."

PROCTOR-SILEX

Today, Proctor-Silex appliances are made by Hamilton Beach/Proctor Silex Inc., a company formed in 1990 when Hamilton Beach Company merged with Proctor-Silex Inc. The company is a subsidiary of Nacco Industries of Cleveland. The Proctor-Silex Company began around 1926 as the Proctor and Schwartz Company. In 1926, Proctor and Schwartz bought the Liberty Company of Cleveland, which had marketed the adjustable temperature iron known as the Liberty Iron. The iron had been developed in 1912 by a 14-year-old boy. In 1929, the first Proctor iron and toaster were introduced, heralding a long line of home appliances, many of which used thermostatic control.

"He virtually invented the consumer -goods industry in America. His products shaped our domestic landscape; he designed everything from meatball makers to hair clippers, electric mixers to garden sprinklers, can openers to baby bottle warmers. Missing from all the standard histories of design and absent from the design and business periodicals of his day, Ivar Jepson was the source of a remarkable stream of products that transformed Sunbeam from a manufacturer of sheep shears into one of the country's major producers of household appliances.

"Jepson was born in November 2, 1903, and grew up on a family farm in Kristianstad in Southern Sweden. He went to Heslehom Technical School to study engineering. After a year's graduate work at the University of Berlin, Jepson set out for America. Enroute to a promised job in North Dakota, he apparently stopped off in Chicago and never went any furthur west. The city's Swedish community provided welcome and anchorage.

"By 1925, Jepson was employed as a draftsman at the Chicago Flexible Shaft Co., renowned for sheep shearing and horse trimming machines. Diversification into home appliances had started in 1910 — though they remained secondary lines. With Jepson's arrival, everything changed. Chicago Flexible Shaft began to be transformed by an astonishing flow of patents in his name, which translated into best selling products. One of the biggest was in 1930, with the introduction of the Sunbeam Mixmaster mixer. Though Jepson did not invent this product, his redesign and upgrading set new standards in kitchen appliances. Other appliances such as irons, can openers, toasters, fans, clocks, electric scissors and waffle irons followed. Even in the depth of the Depression the company turned a profit, and by 1946 the Sunbeam brand was so well known that Chicago Flexible Shaft was officially re-named the Sunbeam Corporation.

"Chief engineer from 1932, and Vice President of Research & Development from 1956 until his retirement in 1963, Jepson's work for Sunbeam offers an outstanding example of consistent design-led market performance. Jepson's

ideas came from constant observation and conversation, followed by concentrated thought. Many of his product designs were created with labor-saving, or more flexible operation, in mind. His electric fry pan, one of first on the market, was square to hold more food, had a temperature control in the handle, and could be plugged in anywhere. "In 1950, Jepson's immediate superior was the president of Sunbeam, Barney Bernard Graham, with whom he had a close and informal relationship. Graham left the company in 1956 following a boardroom coup. Sunbeam began to change with a new emphasis on corporate hierarchy; lines of responsibilities were established, stricter financial controls were introduced and a market-research section was developed. Jepson was pressured to expand his department to cope with growth in other product categories such as power tools and gardening equipment. All this change was not to Jepson's liking: he preferred to originate ideas, rather than to be the manager of a complex organization over which he had less control. Consumer research was beginning to drive product development. When the emphasis shifted from product quality to bottom line issues of corporate management, finance and marketing, Jepson decided to retire in 1963. 2 years later he died of a heart attack.

"Jepson didn't invent the consumer-goods industry single-handedly: even at Sunbeam there were products that predated his arrival. But his contribution was enormous, significantly expanding the concept of what was appropriate for the home. In his own way, Jepson also refuted the stereotype of designer as stylist, tool of manipulative marketing techniques. He was typical of a whole generation of corporate designers whose work has been generally overlooked in favor of their more glamorous, publicity conscious counterparts in design consultancies. Yet Ivar Jepson contributed as much a Raymond Loewy and Walter Teague towards shaping his age, putting his stamp anonymously on myriad objects that create identity and meaning in our domestic landscape."
—from I.D. Magazine, May/June 1994 .

SUNBEAM

In 1910, the Chicago Flexible Shaft Company (founded in 1897) switched from manufacturing primarily non-electrical farm tools (like sheep shearing machines, hand clippers, and flexible shafts used to propel or balance other tools) to electric appliances. Their first electric tool was the "Princess" electric iron, thought to be one of the earliest electric irons made. The continued success of their electric appliances prompted the company to adopt the brand name "Sunbeam" in its advertisements. In 1930 the company introduced the Sunbeam Mixmaster, which is considered the company's most successful appliance. Despite the hard economic times, Sunbeam products contin-

ued to sell very well. Their line included the Sunbeam Ironmaster Dry Iron, Sunbeam Shavemaster Shaver, the first pop-up toaster, and the first automatic electric coffeemaker.

After World War II, the Chicago Flexible Shaft Company changed its name to the Sunbeam Corporation. It continued to produce appliances such as the popular Sunbeam Egg Cooker (1950), the Sunbeam Controlled Heat Fry Pan (1953), the first electric blanket (1955), and an improved deluxe version of the Mixmaster (1956). Sunbeam made a major move when it acquired the Oster Manufacturing Company in 1960. Sunbeam/Oster is still going strong. Collectors often note that Sunbeam produced some classic designs. Everyone should own a Mixmaster—preferably an old one!

Advertisement showing the Sunbeam Cooker & Deep Fryer, from *Good Housekeeping*, November 1954.

WEST BEND

West Bend Aluminum Company was incorporated in 1911 by seven men, two of whom had previously managed an aluminum factory. The company's first products were a frying pan, a pie pan, a water dipper, and sauce pans. Over the next few years the product line expanded, and sales representatives established the company's products with Sears, Roebuck & Company; Wanamakers; Gimbel Bros.; and other large department stores and mail order firms.

West Bend contributed mess kits and other small items to the military effort in World War I. After the war, West Bend introduced two items of note: the famous "Waterless Cooker," and a new drip coffee maker.

The "Waterless Cooker" is a large aluminum pct with insert pans designed to cook an entire meal over one burner. The lid of the cooker was fitted with clamps that prevented the escape of steam during cooking, enabling meals to be cooked in a very small amount of water. The "Waterless Cooker" evolved into the Flavo-Seal ware line, which adopted the concept to roasters, skillets, and sauce pans. The enormous success of the Flavo-Seal line allowed the company to survive the Depression, and even make a profit.

West Bend's new drip coffee maker is notable because it did not require filter paper. The popularity of the Flavo-Drip led to the Flavo-Perk, a range top percolator.

In 1932, West Bend ventured away from aluminum with a successful new line of copper giftware. This line included beverage sets, ashtrays, serving trays, and mugs.

Advertisement displaying various West Bend products, from *Better Homes & Gardens*, December 1956. After Mirro, West Bend is most often associated with aluminum. . . . this full page ad shows why.

During World War II, West Bend converted to war production like everyone else. They produced over three hundred items under defense contracts, including powder tanks and rocket containers.

West Bend's first postwar product was the "Elgin," a 1 1/4 horsepower outboard motor made exclusively for Sears and manufactured at a new plant. Between 1946 and 1950, West Bend developed a line of small appliances including popcorn poppers and skillets; a line of kitchenware items; and a color finishing process for aluminum. Also at this time, the Flavo-Perk percolator became electric and its name was changed to Flavo-Matic.

The Korean War brought more defense contracts. The company partially converted to war production while continuing limited manufacture for public consumption. In 1961, The West Bend Aluminum Company changed its name to West Bend Company to reflect its use of plastics, copper, steel, and brass in addition to aluminum. West Bend continued to expand, adding new lines of decorative pantryware and insulated serving pieces, as well as new appliances. In 1968, West Bend merged with Rexall Chemical and Drug, which later changed its name to Dart Industries.

WESTINGHOUSE

Owned by the Westinghouse Electric Corporation, the brand name Westinghouse is almost synonymous with electricity. Its founder, George Westinghouse, developed the first AC generator in 1886, the year he established the Westinghouse Electric & Manufacturing Company After much public resistance to AC over DC current, the public was won

A selection of Westinghouse appliances, from the 1950s.

over to AC. In 1896, Westinghouse had installed large AC generators to harness power from Niagara Falls. With the success of the Niagara Falls project, Westinghouse turned to hundreds of other electrical products that would come on to the market in the ensuing years. Westinghouse came out with the first electric fry pan in 1911!

At the 1939 Worlds' Fair in New York, the Westinghouse pavilion was advertising and selling its latest electrical appliance: the Adjust-O-Matic iron. This was the world's first iron that could be set at different temperatures and kept there as long as the user wanted. By the beginning of World War II, Westinghouse kitchen and home appliances were everywhere.

During the war Westinghouse provided numerous technological advances for the armed forces, including electric torpedoes, radar guided guns, and tank gun stabilizers. During the Cold War, Westinghouse equipped the first atomic powered submarine, the USS *Nautilus*, in 1955. Since 1945 the company has been known as the Westinghouse Electric Corporation.

WARING CORPORATION

The Waring Corporation was incorporated in 1937 to exploit the "miracle mixer" commonly called the "Waring Blendor" (spelled blendor by Waring to make the product stand out). Fred Waring, the famous bandleader, had financed the development and marketing of the Blendor and promoted it through his Waring Corporation. The Waring Blendor was enthusiastically received at restaurant and trade shows, and became the "in" thing for bars and restaurants.

Advertisement featuring the Waring "Blendor" by the Waring Corp., from *Good Housekeeping*, October 1954. Waring always spells its blender with an 'o'.

At the same time, Waring struck a contract with General Electric to make the Waring steam iron under the GE name.

Convincing people that the Blendor was useful as something other than a drink mixer was not easy. During the 1950s, Waring introduced colored blenders (1955), an ice crusher attachment (1956), and a coffee grinder attachment (1957). Much time and effort was spent educating the public on using the blendor at home for cooking.

The Waring Corporation was consolidated into the Dynamic Corporation of America in 1956. Dynamic continued to use the trade name "the Waring Blendor."

OTHER MANUFACTURERS

Other companies existed through this period and produced many items...some excellent, some not so good. Little information could be found at this time on the remaining companies, but I hope more will surface in the future.

Camfield—Believed to be part of A. F. Dormeyer Manufacturing Company. In the 1950s, Camfield made a "Blue Ribbon" line of appliances including the Fri-Cook, the Power Mix (a combination mixer and grinder), the Power Mix Jr., a knife and scissors sharpener, the automatic Toast-Maid, and the stainless steel Coffee Maid.

Cory—Manufactured electric kitchen appliances up through the 1960s. A vacuum-style coffee pot, a water pot, and a toaster have been seen.

Dominion Electric Corporation—A subsidiary of Scovill Corporation. An innovative oven-broiler was introduced in 1962. Used in one position, it broils and toasts; turned completely upside-down, it bakes and roasts. Hot plates and waffle irons have been seen most often in the collecting field.

Knapp Monarch Company—In 1931, introduced a group of "Therm-A-Magic" percolators designed to shut off at a pre-determined time and after reaching a pre-determined temperature. In 1935, the company announced its "Tel-A-Matic" toaster with a timing device employing bi-metal construction. This

Advertisement showing appliances for the Cory Corp., from *House & Garden,* December 1961.

Advertisement displaying Redi-Baker by Knapp Monarch, from *Good Housekeeping,* December 1958.

Products of the future by Dominion Electric Co., from a sales brochure circa the early 1960s. Computers for the home were still just talk when these appliances were predicted, and their association with computers, ultrasound, and lasers made these "Jetsons-era" items more fantastic. What ever happened to the laser beam can opener?

device required a definite time for each cycle to heat and cool, and "remembered" to allow more time for a cold toaster and less time for a hot one. Knapp Monarch entered the iron field in 1940 with a "Steam King" iron, and also manufactured an extensive line of portable space heaters. In the late 1950s, Knapp Monarch merged with NESCO. The NESCO line is still active today. The firm is now part of the Hoover Company.

National Stamp and Enameling Company—Produced numerous cookware pieces, most notably saucepots and pans, electric cookers, and roasters under the brand name NESCO. Merged with Knapp Monarch around 1960.

The Aluminum Cooking Utensil Company—Made aluminum cookware, bakeware, and foils marketed under the well-known name "Wear-Ever." In the mid-1930s, Wear-Ever juicers were one of the top competitors in the field. The company entered the giftwares market in the 1930s with their Kensington line of "upscale" aluminum giftware. Kensington ware is much sought after today.

Century Metalcraft Corporation - In the 1930s, the Century Metalcraft Corporation of Chicago was selling, with great success, a line of cookware and serving pieces under the name Silver Seal. These aluminum alloy pieces had textured surfaces and simple design with open handles or black wooden handles if the piece required one. The Silver Seal line was more than likely taken out of production during World War II, but was reincarnated in a new and more interesting look later on. By the late 1940s, Century had released its Guardian Service line. This included most of the basic pieces of the Silver Seal line with changes. The first change was the replacement of metal lids with heavy glass lids embossed with the Guardian knight and crossed battle axes in the glass. Decorative fan-shaped knobs and handles now replaced the plain Silver Seal ones on all glass lids and metal bodies. Changes from the Silver Seal to the

Guardian line included: Discontinued fry pans and use of black wooden handles; additions of footed oval serving tray and large round serving tray; two Silver Seal items, a steak platter and the bail-handled Griddle-grill consolidated into the Griddle broiler for Guardian line; Bakelite handle on coffee pot. Most "junk shoppers" can identify the texture of these pieces and assume they are all from the same line. I hope I have clarified this so you can tell a Silver Seal from a Guardian. Most collectors in this field are already pretty savvy. Pieces in good condition are a valued find and a glass lid is a real prize!

Ekco—The kitchen utensil and "gadget" manufacturer with a history reaching back almost a hundred years. They have been a consistent provider of small kitchen utensils such as spatulas, graters, whisks, ladles, and spoons. Under the Flintware line, Ekco produced cookware and flatware as well as utensils. In the 1950s, the Flintware line was being designed by the noted industrial designer Raymond Loewy. Ekco was acquired by West Bend Company in the 1980s.

Advertisement featuring Flintware by Ekco Products Co., from *Better Homes & Gardens,* December 1956.

Complete Guardian Line circa 1950 by the Century Metalcraft Corp. This line replaced Century Metalcraft Corporation's earlier Silver Seal line of cookware.

CHAPTER 4

Collecting Electric Appliances

IDENTIFYING PIECES BY DESIGN

Style isn't everything, but it sure can help to identify a piece. It is important for collectors to learn the "look" of each era or decade. The excessive ornament on 1920s appliances gave way to the streamlined look of 1930s Art Deco; circular waffle irons were popular until after World War II, when square shapes were introduced; chrome and Bakelite gave way to pastel-colored appliances in the 1950s, and so on. Design and technology changed constantly during these decades, partly in an effort to keep appliances attractive to consumers.

A good way to study these styles (and even get exact year dates) for appliances and various kitchenwares is through old magazine advertisements. These magazines can usually be found bound in volumes at your local library if you live in a large city. Smaller city and town libraries may be able to obtain them through inter-library loans. Magazines popular with housewives are the best: *Good Housekeeping, Parents Magazine, The American Home,* and *Better Homes and Gardens,* and *House Beautiful* are but are few to search through.

DATING PIECES BY PATENT NUMBERS

Turn over almost any appliance and you will see a patent number. Most people think it's the year the appliance was made, but this is not necessarily the case. Also, what if more than one patent number appears? The following simple definitions will help you to understand the realtionship between different patent numbers and the date of the appliance. Let's say we've just turned over an imaginary toaster . . .

Patent Number—Also called Utility Patent. The book *Patent It Yourself* defines it very nicely: "A Utility Patent covers inventions that function in a unique manner to produce a utilitarian result." It gives the inventor the right to exclude others from making, using, or selling the invention claimed in the patent deed for approximately 17 years. The patent is issued at the time the inventor's patent application is approved by the U.S. Patent Office. Getting approval can sometimes take up to two years, depending on the amount of paperwork involved and when the

inventor gets around to filing. In the time period we are considering in this book, the patent number is a seven digit number preceded by "PAT #." It does not show the year (unlike a copyright), except in rare cases. To determine the year of the patent, a patent list is necessary.

Part of the government's list of patent numbers for the years 1935-1965 is provided below. This chart matches each year with the range of patent numbers assigned in that year, showing the first patent number that year. Your patent number will fall between two patent numbers in the chart. Remember, this is *not* necessarily the year in which the toaster was made. If a toaster's design had not changed in ten years, it may bear a 1935 patent number even though it was manufactured in 1945.

PATENT NUMBERS 1935-1965

The numbers listed after each year are the patent numbers issued that year in each category. Refer to these to date your own pieces by their patent numbers.

Year	Patent #	Re-Issue #	Design #
1935	1,985,878	19,409	94,179
1936	2,026,516	19,045	98,045
1937	2,066,309	20,226	102,601
1938	2,104,004	20,610	107,738
1939	2,142,080	20,954	112,765
1940	2,185,170	21,311	118,358
1941	2,227,418	21,683	124,503
1942	2,268,540	21,882	130,989
1943	2,307,007	22,242	134,717
1944	2,338,081	22,415	136,946
1945	2,366,154	22,584	139,862
1946	2,391,856	22,706	143,386
1947	2,413,675	22,827	146,165
1948	2,433,824	22,957	148,267
1949	2,457,797	23,068	152,235
1950	2,492,944	23,186	156,686
1951	2,563,016	23,315	161,404
1952	2,580,379	23,449	165,568
1953	2,624,046	23,612	168,527
1954	2,664,562	23,763	171,241
1955	2,698,434	23,918	173,777
1956	2,728,913	24,105	176,490
1957	2,775,762	24,263	179,467
1958	2,818,567	24,413	181,829
1959	2,866,973	24,584	164,204
1960	2,919,443	24,761	186,973
1961	2,966,881	24,916	189,516
1962	3,015,103	25,107	192,004
1963	3,070,801	25,309	194,304
1964	3,116,487	25,507	197,269
1965	3,163,865	25,707	199,955

What if this imaginary toaster has more than one patent number, all falling within a few years? The lowest number is the original patent. But what are the other numbers? If they are less than 17 years apart, they could not be renewals of an expired patent. Rather, they are the patents granted for required upgrades or improvements of components. Each improvement made in an appliance must be patented separately, in the year of the upgrade. A new type of spring system for raising the toast on our toaster, added in 1948, would have that year's patent number appearing somewhere after the original patent number. The last patent number would show the year of the last "improvement."

After the 17-year limit, though, a number could be the new original patent number. Multiple patent numbers are more common on older appliances, mainly because the technology was changing so rapidly. Appliances were being updated often—but what more can you do to a toaster today?

With a little patience you can get a good approximate date for the toaster—or any other appliance. Sometimes patent numbers appear on the original packaging of utensils and smaller appliances. (One more bit of techno info on patents: **Patent It Yourself** says, "Anyone can apply for a patent as long as they are the true inventor of the invention. Even dead or insane persons may apply through their personal representatives.")

Reissue Patent— This is a patent number issued to replace an earlier patent that contained inadvertent errors, made without deceptive intent. A reissue patent takes the place of the original patent. Reissue patent numbers do not show up often.

Design Patent—is issued for a unique, ornamental visible shape or design of an object of manufacture. The uniqueness of the shape must be purely ornamental or aesthetic; if it is functional, then only a utility patent is proper, even if it also aesthetic. A good way to distinguish between a design and utility patent is to ask the question, "Is the novel feature(s) there for structural or functional reasons, or only for the purpose of ornamentation?" A kitchen clock shaped like a teapot would warrant a design patent. Design patents were issued for 3.5, 7, or 14 years as requested at time of application. This made good sense in the era when decorative design was rapidly changing and even appliances were subjected to the constant re-styling and streamlining of the day. Since 1982, design patents are given only for 14 year intervals. You will find design patents on some appliances, but not all. If you find them, they will at least give you the date(s) when the re-styling took place. They are usually shown as "DES #" or just "D #" preceding the number.

Pat Pend., Pat Pending or **Patent Applied For**— This mark indicates that the inventor has applied for a patent but that it hasn't been fully registered at the time. This is sort of a "watch out" warning to anyone thinking of replicating the item. You will see "Pat. Pend." on many appliances, kitchenware, and utensils.

DATING PIECES BY POSTAL CODES

Zone Codes (1942-1963)—This strictly urban coding system was created during World War II, when huge numbers of rural refugees, migrants, and war workers flooded cities. Many workers were employed at the postal service, where they found it easier to sort by zone code numbers than by locations. The postal service also needed to expand its system to accommodate urban growth. Zone codes started at 1, which designated the center of town, and moved outward to the city limits. The zone code number appeared between the city and state (e.g. Portland 2, Oregon). These zone code numbers now correspond to the last two digits of our modern zip codes.

Zip codes (1963 and after)—Zip codes can also help you date appliances. Ads, recipe booklets, manuals, and promotional material relating to appliances will usually show the company or manufacturer's address. If the familiar five-digit zip code appears with the address, you are looking at pieces made after 1963, the year zip codes were first implemented. Though first officially assigned on July 1, 1963, their use was never actually made mandatory except for 2nd and 3rd class bulk mail.

UNDERWRITERS LABORATORIES

Sometimes you will see a small sticker marked **UL** on the bottom of an appliance (more than likely it has partially or completely worn off). This stands for Underwriters Laboratories, a product safety certification laboratory. The **UL** (as it is known) operates safety certification programs to ascertain that items produced under the service are safeguarded against reasonably foreseeable risks. Field representatives make unannounced visits to factories to countercheck products bearing the **UL** mark. You can not date a piece by the UL mark, as the organization was founded in 1894 and still operates today, but it's nice to know if you come across a sticker or tag and aren't familiar with this highly respected consumer watchdog organization.

CARING FOR & USING VINTAGE APPLIANCES

It is important to approach electrical appliances with caution: you could be subjected to an electric shock or your home could be victim to a blown socket or circuit. Let me assure you that if the magnitude of these incidences were so great as to be a major hazard, this book would (and could) not exist. In the last year I have plugged in about 100 old appliances, most found as-is, and not once did I experience shock or problems with circuits. With a moderate precautions, these problems can be easily avoided. Simply speaking, the smartest thing to do would be to go to an appliance repair and service business that services vintage appliances (see Appliance Repair). Here are some more suggestions on caring for and using your vintage appliances.

• When you get your newly-acquired appliance home, you'll want to plug it in and see if it runs.
• First make sure the appliance is turned off. If there is a switch or indicator dial, Set it to OFF.
• Check the cord - most appliances before the 1960s, had detachable cords with a socket plug at one end and a receptacle to the appliance at the other. If the cord is too deteriorated, toss it and try to find a replacement.
• If the cord is useable, examine it. The cords for vintage appliances were usually rubber or synthetic coated which have gone brittle and cracked with age. Many times you will also find cords with a cloth two-toned woven effect that seems to be slightly iridescent. These came in a handful of black/white, brown/white, brown/tan combinations. One cord I examined under a magnifying glass revealed metallic threads sewn in with the material. These cloth cords are desired by collectors today. The most important cord problem is EXPOSURE OF WIRES. Examine the cord where it enters the plug and receptacle. These spots are most vulnerable to fraying, or wearing away of the covering material. If fraying has occured anywhere on the cord as well, this could indicate wire exposure. Take a good look and if you can see wire exposed, torn, or severed, you will need to repair it first. This could mean anywhere from a patch job with electrical tape to total rewiring. Have someone who knows this sort of repair to do this if you are not sure of the procedure. If the cord is just frayed, you still might want to tape it.
• Plugs and Receptacle—On the plug end, hold the cord and plug and tug slightly, to see if the wiring is tight. Looking down into the plug, check to see if the inside is exposed. This will need to be covered. Dust the insides (dust can cause minor sparking when plugged in) and tighten the two screws with a screwdriver, making sure the two separate wires are not touching. Cover the opening with a cut-out cardboard shape or buy a plug cover at a hardware store. If you end up having to rewire, you will probably go through this whole procedure anyway. Receptacles on vintage appliances were either two pieces that screwed apart at the seams or one molded piece. The two piece kind can be re-wired as for plugs. The molded kind seem un-re-wireable. Older cords have

wider receptacles and the receptacle holes are fatter and larger apart than cords of the late 1950s and on. Not all cords will fit all appliances!
• Most toasters and later appliances (later than the mid-1950s) had attached cords. The above guidelines apply to these type of cords as well.
• Cords are a very important part of an appliance. PLEASE DO NOT yank the cord out of the wall socket by grasping the cord and pulling it. I did this with an old 1940s space heater and it cost me dearly in replacing a circuit! Always pull at the plug.
• Clean your appliance! Besides the cleaning information in the introduction, other suggestions apply. Open doors on bottoms of toasters and clean out old crumbs. Items that came in contact with oil and grease (like fryers, waffle irons, and roasters) are likely to need some cleaning—check for built up grease around knobs, handles, and feet. Mixers and blenders offer little cleaning problems. Most relatively clean appliances can be "refreshed" rather easily. Don't be lazy and wait—clean your appliance after you use it.
• NEVER leave older electrical appliances unattended for long periods of time when they are turned on.
• NEVER plug too many vintage appliances into one socket at the same time. (I wouldn't even gamble on two, if you're unsure of the wiring!) Regardless of whether you live in an older home with adequate wiring or you live in a new home with wiring up to modern standards, you are taking a chance of blowing a fuse. Technologically less "energy-efficient" than modern appliances, vintage appliances can draw more power from a circuit. Though this has been going on since electric appliances were first made, use common sense and most problems can be avoided.

APPLIANCE REPAIR

Fortunately, most older appliances can be repaired. Unless you are a real handyman or woman around the house or familiar with electronics, don't try this at home, kids! Search the yellow pages of your city and don't give up—you will eventually find a small-appliance service center that can do repair jobs on your old favorites. They can also clean the appliance and repair minor or major parts if necessary. Motors are the most expensive parts to replace, costing about $30 to $50 to repair or replace. Heating elements, simple gears, plugs, and switches should cost under $30 to repair. Try to find a repair shop that scrounges for old appliances and uses the original parts from these to replace and repair the ones you bring in. This is not always possible, but it is preferable; new parts are not always considered well-made in the appliance trade. It's also good to take your appliance in for cleaning and service yearly, if you can. Appliances with motors need oiling if used frequently. The repair shop here in Portland, Oregon, offers UPS shipping so folks in rural areas can ship in their prized appliances for repair. Such a deal!!

For the serious collector or the owner of a particularly choice appliance in need of attention, I suggest an appliance restoration business in New England called "Appliance Rebirthing." The owner and operator, David Wiener, describes the function of the business as "authentic and fantasy restorations, replacement parts, attachments, and service for vintage electrical appliances." He will also supply color copies of the corresponding owners manuals from his extensive collection. Fees run under $100 for most smaller repairs and service. Restorations, including replating, will go over $100. **Appliance Rebirthing** of Hartford, Connecticut, is well known for their historical appreciation and knowledge of vintage appliances. They can be reached at 330 Laurel Street, Suite #401, Hartford, CT 09105-2708 or (203) 547-1289.

1940s Hamilton Beach model G food mixer. Restored and chrome finished by Appliance Rebirthing! In the collection of R. Comer.

REMOVING BAKED-ON GREASE

In your search for older appliances, you will eventually encounter the dreaded "baked-on grease." All cookware and most appliances that come in contact with heat or have a heating component in them can fall victim to this. Over the years, cooking grease and heat can form an orangy-black glaze that seems impossible to get off. Unfortunately, in many cases, it cannot be entirely removed. The following are the best pieces of advice I can offer for removing baked-on grease:

• "409"-type all-purpose cleaners work, kind of, but require excessive scrubbing which will scratch the metal so much as to ruin the shiny finish on chrome, nickel, and stainless steel. You really have to rub to get the hardest baked-on grease off.
• Brasso seems to work well if applied and left on a few minutes, but ultimately you will need to scrub the tough parts off.
• An industrial strength oven cleaner works somewhat better than the commercial brands and cuts down on the time and scrubbing. Applying for a few minutes or more to let the cleaner soak in helps considerably. There are all kinds that can be purchased at janitorial supply houses selling to the public. Be careful when you use them as they are more toxic and concentrated. Wear rubber gloves and work in a ventilated area.
• Here's a final trick that sometimes works on electric appliances: IF your appliance is working, turn it on! Let it heat up fairly hot, and then turn it off. The heat softens the grease and in some cases the baked-on grease comes right off with cleaning, except the most imbedded stuff. However, the metal is now extremely hot and you can burn yourself while cleaning, so clean carefully! In fact, you can use the applied heat method to clean any non-electric kitchen item, including pots, pans, and utensils. In these cases, submerge them in very hot water (be careful of plastic components like handles and knobs). The heat will soften the grease and you can proceed as above for cleaning, with fairly successful results.

As you see, there is no easy cure. I hope my suggestions will help—keep trying and good luck!

CHAPTER 5
The Appliances

A Note on reading patent numbers in the captions: If only one "year" number is shown, that was the one patent number on the appliance. If I list a range of year numbers (e.g. 1942-1950) this indicates that there are two or more patent numbers listed on the piece. I don't list every patent number on a piece in each caption. If there were more than two, the two year numbers I list are the earliest and latest patent numbers shown, with others falling in between. Patents can be confusing and one can only speculate sometimes on an exact date of manufacture. Some appliances have only design numbers, others have Pat Ped. and others no patent at all!

BLENDERS

Blenders came on the scene much later than most kitchen appliances. In 1932, the Greene Manufacturing Company was producing mixers for the use

"Osterizer" blender. *See related advertisements on pages 159 and 160.*

"Kenmore" electric blender by Sears in white base. *Courtesy of Jim Sutherland.* $20-40

"as a blender in the macerating of fruits and vegetables so as to reduce them to a fluid state." This was developed by Stephen Poplawski, who had been developing and marketing commercial drink mixers, in cruder forms, since 1916, the year of his first patent. Concurrent to this, a man named Fred Osius asked the bandleader Fred Waring to back his blender idea. In 1938, the Waring "Blendor" made its appearance. The Waring Blendor and the Osterizer were the two blenders that struggled most to gain acceptance in the American home as more than just a "drink mixer." As you search for a vintage blender, seek out these two classic examples. The Osterizer's base has a smooth beehive look that is particularly appealing in chrome, and the Waring Blendor's base looks like a Buck Rogers rocket base. Remember: the more speeds (starting with off and on) the blender has, the more recent it is. In light of that, it might be worthwhile to find the first push-button blenders from the early 1960s. My attempts to find vintage blenders usually turn up parts, so I guess I could assemble one Frankenstein-style.

BROILERS

Broiling is probably the oldest form of cooking, known primarily in its pre-historic form as "raw meat on end of stick held over fire." Electric broiling is a little more recent—the first table appliance to be designed specifically for broiling was invented and marketed in 1916. However, the first table broiler of the type that would be generally regarded as standard was introduced in 1937 by the International Appliance Company. The "Broil King" would become International's hottest item, and the company would later be credited with major improvements on this appliance.

At the same time, other companies joined the competition. Manning Bowman introduced a table broiler they claimed was somehow smokeless. The Rival Manufacturing Company came out with an "electric steak platter," which it later developed into a more traditional broiler.

The first table broiler equipped with a rotisserie was sold by the little known Rotissimat Corporation in 1946 for the price of $50. The "Rotissimat" was promoted in poultry shops and early supermarkets, where they roasted chickens to demonstrate the appliance. Unfortunately, women wanted to buy just the roasted chickens, not the machine. It is supposed that this was the beginning of the commercial chicken roasting concept now found in supermarkets and other food stores! In 1954, the company liquidated and got out of the broiler business.

Other companies were starting to produce broilers. In 1962, S.W. Farber Inc. announced the revolutionary "Open Hearth" broiler/rotisserie, which for the first time made it possible to broil at the table without a hood over the food.(Sounds messy to me!) The mess factor was mitigated somewhat by the appearance of the self cleaning broiler in 1970.

Electric broiler by Regal Co.
$20-30

Electric broiler marked "Manning Bowman."
$25-35

Electric broiler by Mirro Corp.
$20-30

COFFEE POTS

The earliest coffee pots were made of tin, or sometimes of copper or pewter. After the appearance of porcelain enamel for cookware in America during the 1870s, this new material became the favorite for coffee pots. Porcelain enamel held sway until the turn of the century, when the advent of electric pots made nickel-plating popular.

The first electric percolator was introduced in 1908 by Landers, Frary & Clark under their "Universal" trade name. The "Universal" percolator had a remarkable innovation called the cold water pump. In ordinary percolators then just beginning to be manufactured, the element had to heat all the water in the pot to about 190 degrees before it would "perk." The Universal model was designed with a small well or recess in the base, around which the heating element was brazed. Thus the concentrated heat on a small quantity of water started perking action in two to three minutes. The cold water pump percolator quickly gained fame (and sales), promptly outmoding all ordinary models.

Early electric coffee pots were elegant serving items, usually silver or nickel-plated. They were styled to complement late Victorian furnishings, particularly of the dining room. As time progressed , the coffee pot became sleeker, chrome-plated, and stylish with Art Deco leanings.

By 1937, S.W. Farber Inc. featured the "Coffee Robot" that "Does about everything but buy the coffee." This somewhat industrial-looking vacuum-type brewer made the coffee, shut off the current when it was finished, and used a thermostat control to keet it hot indefinitely. The success of the "Coffee Robot"

led many cooking utensil manufacturers into the percolator business. One of them, the Aluminum Goods Manufacturing Company (now the Mirro Corporation) could boast of producing well over 50% of all the electric percolators in the country during the 1920s and 1930s.

The same years saw another variation on the percolator theme—separate bases containing the heating element. Possibly influenced by the newly released Silex Coffee Pot, many companies produced their own separate base percolators. Among these companies was Sunbeam, whose 7-cup, vacuum-type "Maxwelton Braes" coffee maker, introduced in 1935, is a classic in design.

Electric coffee pot with burner. Pot marked "Silex," burner marked "GE.," 1933-1939. *Courtesy of Old Town Antique Mall, Portland Oregon.* $20-30

Electric coffee pots: (left) by Westinghouse, 1926; (right) by the Forman Family, urn-shaped, chromium on brass. $15-30 each

Electric coffee pots: (left) aluminum with Bakelite handles and knobs, marked "Royal Family Housewares"; (right) aluminum with wood handle, urn-shaped, marked "Montgomery Ward & Co."
$15-40 each

Electric Coffee pot: Chrome and Bakelite reads on bottom: "Jet-O-Matic, Homemakers Guild of America Corporation. Mfg. by M. H. Graham Corp. Minn. Minnesota".
$20-35.

Electric coffee pots: (left) "Superfast" by Farberware, egg-shaped, 1958-1973; (right) "Automatic Percolator" by General Electric, egg-shaped, brown Bakelite handle.
$10-20 each

Electric Coffee pots: Three stages of Universal electric coffee pots: (left) brown Bakelite handles and feet, marked "Universal," 1939; (center) marked "Coffeematic by Universal"; (right) different style handle.
$15-30 each

Electric Coffee pots: (left) "Flavo Matic" by West Bend, in colored aluminum, silo-shaped; (right) "Automatic Percolator" by General Electric, oval, unusual. $25-50 (West Bend); $20-35 (GE)

Advertisement for "CoffeeMaster" by Sunbeam, from *Good Housekeeping*, May 1953.

"Automatic Electric Hurri-Hot Electri-Cup" water pot by Dormeyer. $10-15

"Flavo Matic" electric coffee pot by West Bend, with brown Bakelite handles and feet. $10-20

"Coffeemaster" electric coffee pot by Sunbeam, two-tiered. Desirable.
$20-50

West Bend electric coffee pot with black Bakelite handles.
$10-20

Two-tiered electric coffee pot in chrome, by the Cory Corp. *Courtesy the collection of David Kohl.*
$30-60

"Coffeemaker" electric coffee pot by Presto, completely immersible, 1970.
$10-20

DEFROSTERS

When I first came upon one of these a few years back, I had no idea what it meant to do except heat up. Then I found one in its original box. These items, enclosed heaters with a handle, were used to hasten defrosting of a freezer before self-defrosting freezers came about in the 1960s. I still don't understand how it melted the ice without getting water on the heating element.

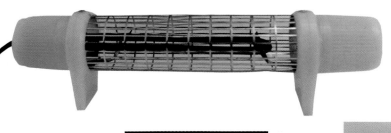

Electric defroster by Cory Corp.
$10-15

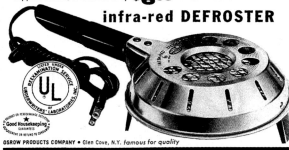

Advertisement for infra-red defroster, from *Good Housekeeping*, December 1962.

Electric defroster of aluminum with a wood handle, marked "Howell Co."
$10-15

Electric defrosters: (top) anodized aluminum, wood handle, Shane Mfg. Company; (bottom) aluminum, plastic handle, Nu-Rod Inc.
$10-15 each

Fry Pans

In olden days when cooking was done at the fireplace, frying pans had to have an extra long handles to keep the cook from getting fried along with the food.

"Controlled Heat Automatic Frypan" by Sunbeam, des# 1930. These fry pans can also be found with pastel-colored handles and matching trim.
$10-20

In the 1890s, the non-electric precursor to the modern electric frypan was having its heyday. Known as the chafing dish, this utensil was a pot or pan which fit into a lower pan of hot water, all supported in a holder over a flame below. The flame kept the water at a simmer and all sorts of slow cooking foods from soups to fondues could be made in it. (some dishes were made in the kitchen and served *from* the chafing dish) Chafing dishes were not only popular for table-side cooking in restaurants but considered the "in" thing in many homes as well. (the chafing dish did fall out of favor but was rediscovered in the 1950s, an era of informal dining)

In 1911, the Westinghouse Company caused quite a sensation when it introduced the electrified version of the chafing dish.It was made of sheet steel,was 6 inches in diameter and had the heating element built into its base. When it was turned over it could double as a hotplate.

Strangely, nearly half a century would elapse before anything more would be done with the electric fry pan. The main problem was developing a dependable heat control, without which electric fry pans would have no advantage over ordinary fry pans. Finally in 1953, Sunbeam introduced an unusual square, cast aluminum "Automatic Frypan" with controlled heat and a fry guide right on the handle to take the guesswork out of temperatures. The fry pan market started to sizzle.

In 1954, S.W. Farber Inc. developed a detachable heat control feature (called the "Probe") that could be used on all items in their line. By its very nature, the "Probe" made the appliance completely immersible in water. At the same time, Farber released its own fry pan. Whereas most other pans were square and made of aluminum, theirs was round and made of stainless steel.

One of the first electric kitchen appliances to go "Teflon" was the fry pan.

"Electric Skillet" by GE in turquoise base with glass top. Unusual.
$50-75

Electric fry pan (top), buffet server-fryer (bottom) with late 1950s styling by Mirro Corp., from a sales brochure.

HOT PLATES

The principle of obtaining heat from electricity was developed in the 1840s by an English scientist. By 1890, an early form of hot plate, known as a table stove, was available. By the 1920s, table stoves with the name "Torrid" were on the market, along with brands by Westinghouse, GE and Universal. The Liberty Gauge and Instrument Company turned out a "Hotspot" hotplate in 1921 for $3.85.

By the 1930s, hot plates were being seen in the ubiquitous chrome with Art Deco styling (the beehive or steeped ring shape being most popular), two burner sets, and hot plate/ coffee pot combos.

The 1940s brought a style of hot plates that looked like they escaped from a chemist's lab! Hot plates were originally not meant to replace the kitchen range, be it coal, wood or gas. They were meant for light cooking (like a chafing dish) at such places as the breakfast table.

Electric hot plate in white porcelain enamel, 9" x 12", marked "Samson United Corp. Rochester, NY."
$15-25

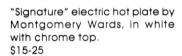

"Signature" electric hot plate by Montgomery Wards, in white with chrome top.
$15-25

"Buffet Queen" electric hot plate by Cory, with two burners and Bakelite handles.
$15-25

Electric hot plates: (left) "Automatic Heat-Rite Base" by Sears, 1960s; (right) "Electrical Trivet" by West Bend.
$10-15 each

Electric hot plates: Metal body / ceramic tile inset with Pennsylvania Dutch motifs marked "Garth Prods. Inc."
$10-15

Electric hot plates: (left) "Two Heater Electric Stove" by Cory Corporation, Bakelite handle; (right) "Hotpoint" by GE, Bakelite handles.
$10-15 each

Electric hot plates: (left) metal body/ceramic top with kitchen designs, marked "Garth Prods. Inc."; (right) plastic body/metal top, marked "All States Wire & Metal Prods."
$10-15 each

PRESSING IRONS

One of the earliest pressing irons on record in modern times is a box-like structure which held hot charcoal. NOT a good idea!

Then came irons which were designed to hold hot pieces of cast iron. These were heated and put in the iron to use while you heated up the next bunch of pieces,sort of like rechargeable batteries.When stoves started to replace the fireplace for cooking, someone had the ingenious idea of casting irons in one piece and heating them on the stove—a great improvement. They called it the "sadiron," not out of deference to the poor housewives who had to lift these things, but because "sad" meant compact or heavy.

When gas was burned in the home in the 19th century, there were gas lights, then gas ranges, and then—gas pressing irons! The gas iron was a potential hazard, but housewives preferred them (hazards and all) over the cumbersome sadirons. Alcohol and gasoline burning irons were also appearing at this time.

"Steam-O-Matic" electric pressing iron, marked "A Titeflex product of the Waverly Tool Co." *Courtesy of Old Town Antique Mall, Portland Oregon.*
$15-30

Electric irons: (left) "Ironmaster" by Sunbeam, 1935-1941; (right) GE, 1931-1944.
$35-45 (Sunbeam); $15-25 (GE)

Advertisement for "2 in 1 Iron" by General Electric, from *Good Housekeeping,* March 1952.

Electric pressing iron by General Electric.
$15-25

Electric irons marked "Landers, Frary, and Clark (Universal)."
$15-25

Electric irons: (left) General Mills, rests on side, unusual; (right) "Champion Automatic Speed Iron" by Proctor Electric Co. in brown Bakelite.
$25-35 (General Mills); $15-25 (Proctor)

Advertisement for "American Beauty" iron by American Electrical Heater Co., from *Better Homes & Gardens*, October 1952. The American Beauty is one of the earliest irons to be manufactured for consumers.

Electric irons marked "Landers, Frary, and Clark (Universal)," 1924-1938.
$15-25

Finally, the electric iron emerged. In 1905, the Pacific Electric Heating Company sold electric laundry irons. At the same time, the American Electric Heater Company sold electric irons to the laundry and tailoring trades. In 1912, they released their famous "American Beauty" iron for household use. The adjustable automatic heat control iron arrived courtesy of the Liberty Gauge and Instrument Company in 1926.

Electric steam irons had already been produced for the trade, but the first steam irons for household use didn't appear until the late 1920s. The "Steam-O-Matic" made its debut in 1938 as the first over-the-top, good quality steam iron. Many others followed, and consumers soon were firmly convinced of the advantages of the steam iron.

After World War II, improvements followed one after another: the use of tap water instead of the mandatory distilled water, the travel steam iron (1953), the "replaceable parts" iron (1963), and the Teflon coated iron (1965).

MIXERS

Hamilton Beach Manufacturing Company is credited with marketing the first cake batter mixer before 1920, a time during which the company was making drink mixers for commercial use. In 1926, Air-O-Mix Inc. released the "Whip All," the first combination base-mounted and/or portable mixer. This set the standard for all mixers from that time on, including the "Dormeyer household beater" in 1927 and the "Polar Cub" hand mixer in different sizes made by A. C. Gilbert Company (famous for its "Erector" sets). (Gilbert also made a special orange juicer for the California Fruit Growers Exchange. Products from the Gilbert Company, especially the orange juicer, are considered rare. They would be a choice find for any appliance fancier.)

The mixer industry received a huge shot in the arm when The Chicago Flexible Shaft Company (Sunbeam) introduced its "Mixmaster" in 1931. Advertised extensively and promoted at every opportunity with demonstrations in key department stores, the "Mixmaster became extremely popular and somewhat of a mixer standard in women's minds. To say that the "Mixmaster" is an appliance classic is an understatement. The design has changed over the years, but the quality has not. This is great news for collectors—most older Mixmasters you find will still be working.

After World War II, mixers benefitted from technological advances such as small motors and electronic controls. By the 1960s the hand held portable mixer, now lightweight, would eventually outpace the base-mounted versions in sales; it needed less counter space, and accomodated changes in eating habits and diminished need.

Advertisement for Sunbeam "Mixmaster," from *Good Housekeeping,* November 1954.

"Mixmaster" Model 12 electric mixer by Sunbeam in pink. Desirable.
$80-120

"Mixmaster" Model 12 electric mixer by Sunbeam in white, 1940s-1950s.
$35-65

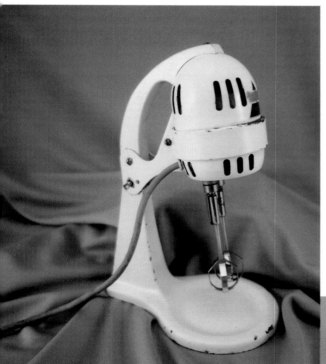

Advertisement for "Mixer" and "Mixette" by Hamilton Beach, from *Better Homes & Gardens*, October 1952.

Mary Dunbar Handymix by Chicago Electric Mfg. Co.
$20-40

Hand held electric mixers: (left) "Dormey" by Dormeyer; (right) "Sunbeam Jr." in yellow by Sunbeam. *Dormeyer courtesy of Palookaville, Portland, Oregon.*
$10-12 (Dormeyer); $25-50 (Sunbeam)

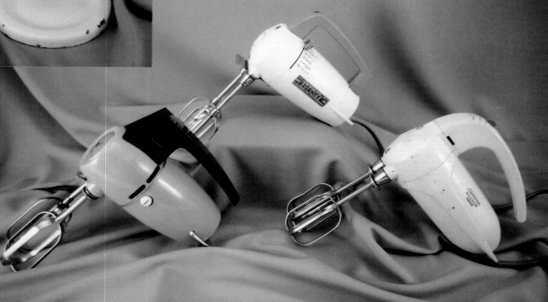

TOASTERS

"When a toaster's carriage-lowering lever is depressed, it closes a switch that turns on the heating element. As the bread toasts, a heat-sensitive bimetallic arm bends and trips a solenoid switch, whose position is set by the light/dark lever. The solenoid lets the carriage pop up, turning off the heating elements at the same time. To keep the toast from being thrown out, the dash pot—a spring-loaded cylinder with a vacuum action—slows the rise of the carriage and delivers the finished piece(s) of toast."
—*Time/Life Home Repair & Improvement*, 1976

Technically speaking, that's how it all happens. Ever since bread met heat, it has been certain that humankind and toast will ne'er be parted. The first regularly manufactured toasters in this country were designed to sit over a coal stove or gas burner and hold four slices of bread tilted towards the center.

Around 1910, Westinghouse announced the release of its electric "toaster stove." The next two decades witnessed considerable progress as manufacturers mastered the handling of electricity for household tasks. Toasters were slowly upgraded until 1926, when the newly incorporated McGraw Electric Company released the "Toastmaster" automatic toaster—a great improvement. The dial was set to the desired type of toast, and the toaster then operated until it automatically shut off. Success of the automatic toaster concept set other companies to emulate it.

More improvements were made in the 1930s and 1940s, including Knapp Monarch's "Tel-A-Matic" model with bi-metal construction (1935) and Sunbeam's bi-metal operated "radiant control" (1949), which allowed the bread to lower automatically and emerge as toast automatically.

After that, there were few new developments in the toaster market until 1956, when General Electric introduced its "Toast-R-Oven." The toaster-oven enjoyed great success in the 1960s and 1970s, but fell out of favor with the advent of microwaves and other 1980s innovations.

Electric toasters: (left) Westinghouse, brown mottled Bakelite base, 1936-1946; (right) GE, brown Bakelite base, 1935-1944, des# 1942. *Westinghouse from the kitchen of Pete and Jackie Dyrhaug; GE courtesy the collection of Jayme Hagen, Portland, Oregon.* $40-65 each

"Toast-O-Lator" by the Toastolator Co. Rare. The novel conveyor belt approach to toasting bread came to a halt after problems with the conveyor belt surfaced. What we are left with is a marvelous Art Deco beauty. The one pictured still works; you can watch your toast go by through a little glass porthole on the side. *Courtesy the collection of Jayme Hagen, Portland Oregon.* $90-175

"Universal" electric toaster with brown Bakelite base, by Landers, Frary & Clark. *Courtesy the collection of Jayme Hagen, Portland Oregon.* $30-50

TOASTERS ARE SOCIAL CLIMBERS

"Toasters are social climbers in the world of household gadgets. Often living in the dining room rather than the kitchen, they feel the need to dress up. Most of them efficiently engineered external bodies of sheet metal and plastic, with appropriate and expressive shapes which are entirely able to stand on their own merits; but most of them have taken the next deplorable step in adding tasteless decoration on the otherwise clean forms. These bits of ornament are usually incised lines in the toaster's side, and range from pseudo-monograms through floral curlicues to quill-penmanship exercises and modernistic patterns of the worst sort.

"Two toasters are worth noting. The Camfield, the best of the group design-wise, has bravely eliminated all decoration and has also come up with a more interesting shape than the others. Corners are more sharply curved than sides, providing firmer modulations of form which are much more interesting than the soft shape of other toasters. The Sunbeam, with an ingenious new mechanical wrinkle (the bread raises and lowers itself automatically), is different in form because the bread is placed crosswise instead of lengthwise. Its form is firm rather than soft, but it is guilty of bad decoration on the side.

"Those manufacturers producing automatic and non-automatic toasters have apparently given most of their design attention to the automatics. Many of the non-automatic toasters are clumsier in shape, and the decoration is even more prevalent and also clumsier. To be sure the problems are different,but there is no reason why a straightforward approach couldn't produce simpler and better designs in this class."

— *by Eliot Noyes, who certainly had a "thing" about superfluous decoration on toasters, from Consumer Reports, November 1949.*

Model T-9 electric toaster by Sunbeam. A classic! This model has been seen on some contemporary cereal and breakfast commercials on TV, and there is a rumor that Sunbeam is planning to reissue it because of nostalgic popularity. *Courtesy the collection of Jayme Hagen, Portland Oregon.*
$50-75

The beautiful *Camfield* is truly a Blue Ribbon Toaster. Fully automatic, with exclusive "Equa-Therm" which times toast exactly to individual taste, despite current variation. This achievement crowns Camfield engineers' long experience in developing fine electric appliances. Among other features are automatic pop-up, finger-tip release, color selector and hinged crumb tray. To give or to possess, the Camfield is indeed *something very special!*

CAMFIELD
AUTOMATIC TOASTER

Camfield Manufacturing Company, Grand Haven, Mich. *In Canada,* Addison Industries, Ltd., Toronto

Advertisement for toaster by Camfield Mfg.Co., from *Good House-keeping,* June 1948.

"Fostoria" automatic pop-up toaster by McGraw Electric Co.
$35-50

"Automatic Toaster" by Camfield, 1933-1945. *Courtesy the collection of Jayme Hagen, Portland Oregon.*
$35-50

"Toastwell" electric toaster. Three people have noted that this toaster looks like an old AirStream trailer; one has said it is shaped like a loaf of bread. *Courtesy the collection of Jayme Hagen, Portland Oregon.* $40-60

"Radiant Control" electric toasters, both by Sunbeam, 1945-1958, des# 1951. $30-60 each

"Toastmaster" electric toaster by McGraw Electric Co., 1936-1945. *From the singular collection of Brenda Fitzgerald and Alex, Xan, and Keller Gordon.* $20-35

Electric toaster by Westinghouse, 1935-1942. *Courtesy of Pete and Jackie Dyrhaug.*
$45-60

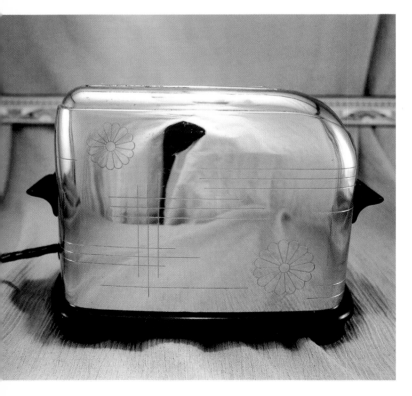

Electric toaster by McGraw Electric Co., 1929-1938, des# 1932.
$35-50

"Toastmaster" electric toaster by McGraw Electric Co., 1929-1942.
$35-50

what's new from General Electric

New DeLuxe Toast-R-Oven* toasts anything...even bakes!

EASIEST TOASTING. When toast is done, door opens, tray slides out automatically. Practically hands the toast to you!

*Trademark of General Electric Company

NEW HEAT CONTROL. Adjusts automatically to any kind of bread. Note the "Brown Top Side" control. Great for muffins.

What's for toast?

Thin slices? Thick slabs? French bread? Garlic bread? Raisin bread? Brown bread? General Electric's DeLuxe Toast-R-Oven toasts *anything*. See? It loads from the front—makes toast easier to reach!

Bakes, too! A flip of the switch and there's your handy controlled-heat oven. Look for the General Electric DeLuxe Toast-R-Oven at your dealer's today. General Electric Co., Portable Appliance Dept., Bridgeport 2, Connecticut.

Progress Is Our Most Important Product

GENERAL ⊕ ELECTRIC

IT BAKES, TOO! Rolls, cookies, frozen meat pies and desserts, even potatoes and meat loaf! Just set desired baking heat.

Advertisement for the Toast-R-Oven by General Electric, from *The Saturday Evening Post*, 1961. The old broiler eventually evolved into the famous toaster oven, as illustrated by this early model.

Tea Kettles

Electric tea kettles were first exhibited at the Chicago World's Fair in 1893. By 1900, Landers, Frary & Clark were offering their version. The example shown is by Sunbeam. It was made in Canada, and dates from the 1940s to 1950s. No other examples have been seen, leading me to suspect that this item was more popular in the early days of electric appliances. The closest I have come is the Dormeyer water pot.

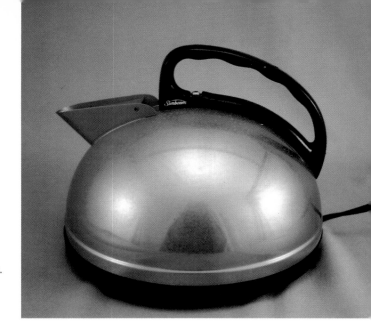

Electric teakettle by Sunbeam, made in Canada. $40-60

Waffle Irons

Long-handled waffle irons and wafer irons were used over the hearth fire in early American kitchens. In 1865, Griswold Manufacturing Company, producers of iron kitchenware, sold a waffle iron. It was one of their most popular items (and probably the reason why we call this appliance an *iron*). Before the first electric waffle irons appeared, early electric griddle cake (pancake) cookers were advertised, beginning around 1905.

One of the first electric waffle irons was advertised by Landers, Frary, & Clark in 1918. The next year, a competitor released a waffle iron with a heat indicator.

By the 1920s and 1930s, griddle cake cookers went out of favor and waffle irons gained in popularity. They were usually round or rectangular shape, the latter sometimes having two lids, allowing the removal of one waffle while the other was cooking. Look for names like Manning-Bowman, Samson, Sears, Hotpoint, and McGraw on this era of waffle irons.

The 1940s and 1950s saw the appearance of the larger square waffle iron (more waffle for your money), the reversible waffle iron/sandwich grill grid, and the removable grid for easier cleaning. By the way, during World War II, waffle irons were considered one of the more practical appliances to have, because waffles used non-rationed food items.

Illustration of waffle iron, from *Good Housekeeping*, June 1951.

"White Cross" electric waffle iron by National Stamping and Electric Works, round with Art Deco styling.
$40-60

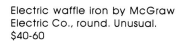

Electric waffle iron by McGraw Electric Co., round. Unusual.
$40-60

"Hotpoint" electric waffle iron by GE, round with black wooden handles and knobs.
$40-60

Electric Waffle irons: Rectangular and round models, both by Dominion in similar styling. $35-60 each

Electric waffle iron, chrome with Bakelite handles, rectangular. $30-40

Electric waffle iron, chrome with white Bakelite handles, by Manning Bowman & Co., 1924. $45-65

Electric waffle iron by Westinghouse with black Bakelite handles and incised leaf design.
$30-45

Electric Waffle iron: Chrome and Bakelite marked "Universal - the trademark known in every home". $35-50. 1935 Pat #.

Interchangeable grill trays that go with the 1936 Universal waffle iron.
$8-12.

Electric sandwich grill "Samson" by Samson United Co., with plain wood handles.
$40-60

Advertisement for Universal "Cook-A-Matic," from *Good House-keeping*, June 1952.

"Samson" electric sandwich grill by Sansom United Co., 1932-1936.

Electric waffle iron/ grill: (left) "Dominion" by Dominion Electric Co., square with brown Bakelite handles; (right) "Fostoria" by McGraw Electric Co., square, 1929, 1941.
$35-55 (Dominion); $30-45 (Fostoria)

OTHER APPLIANCES

Electric popcorn popper, brick red and tan, with crank to turn kernels. Made by U.S. Mfg. Co. *Courtesy of Urban Edge, Portland, Oregon.*
$15-25

Popcorn popper with late 1950s styling by Mirro Corp., from a sales brochure.

Electric popcorn poppers: (left) Kenmore by Sears and Roebuck; (right) Fostoria by McGraw Electric Co., with glass top.
$10-20 (Kenmore); $15-25 (Fostoria)

"Fri-Well" electric deep fryer by Dormeyer, 1952.
$25-45

Advertisement for "Fryryte" deep fryer by Dulane Inc., from *Better Homes & Gardens*, October 1952.

Electric cooker/roaster marked "Dominion," with attached cord.
$25-45

Electric cooker/roaster by Sunbeam, "1952" on front.
$35-50

Electric roaster by Westinghouse. *Photo by Chuck Meyer.*
$35-55

Roaster "Heat-wel" by Welko Inc.
$35-50

1920s era electric appliances (left to right): waffle iron by Hotpoint, Edison Electric Co. Inc.; "L&H Turnsit Toaster" by Lindemann & Hoverson Co. *Courtesy of Jim Sutherland, Portland Oregon.*

Electric egg cooker with four pieces (egg trivet, poaching insert, body and lid with plastic measure), by Sunbeam, 1944, des# 1951.
$25-45

"Peel King" electric knife with different attachments, by S&H Mfg. Co., in box, 1961.
$10-20

Electric can opener/knife sharpener with pink and chrome body, by the Udico Electric Co., 1957-1960.
$35-55

CHAPTER 6
Metal Kitchenware & Related Items

This country, it has been said, was built on iron and steel. Great bridges, hurling skyscrapers, spanning vast coasts, etc. Here, we will limit our scope to the more mundane but no less fascinating field of non-electric but metal kitchen items of decades past. The scope of items is amazing, ranging from the popular bread boxes and canisters, to an exotic array of iron rests, hot pads, utensils, recipe boxes and ice cube trays. Try to notice as you collect the gradual replacing of metal objects by plastic kitchenware, which was just being made to consumers in mass quantities after the war. Watch as metal canisters, dustpans, gadgets, serving trays, and ice cube trays "go plastic" and you will see less metal kitchen items available today than there were years ago.

There is truly still a wealth of items available at sensible prices for every collector in this field today. The items of the 1960s are just being discovered by the ever-diligent, particularly early 1960s items featuring a more sleeker, aerodynamic styling than the 1950s versions. Collecting this period will take a high tolerance to the color Avocado.

BREAD BOXES

Red and white bread box with loaf of bread and tulips. Courtesy of Old Town Antique Mall, Portland Oregon.
$10-20

Bread box with tulip decals, marked "Empeco/National Can Company."
$8-12

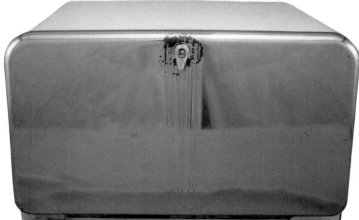

Pink bread box with copper front, bread board inside lid, marked "Beauty Box by Lincoln."
$12-25

Aluminum roll-top bread box, marked "Maid of Honor." $15-30

Yellow bread box with white top. *Courtesy of Old Town Antique Mall, Portland Oregon.* $15-20

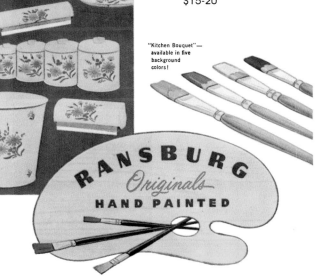

"Kitchen Bouquet" — available in five background colors!

Advertisement showing various metal kitchen items made by Ransburg, from *Better Homes & Gardens,* October 1952. The pattern is called "Kitchen Bouquet" and is advertised as "refrigerator type enamel — baked on for permanence."

CAKE KEEPERS

Aluminum cake keeper, marked "Mirro." Courtesy *of Old Town Antique Mall, Portland Oregon.*
$10-12

Aluminum cake keeper, yellow, marked "West Bend."
$6-10

Colored aluminum cake keeper, marked "West Bend."
$10-15

Square cake keeper in colored aluminum, marked "West Bend," with white plastic handle.
$12-18

Colored aluminum cake keeper, with etched texture and wooden acorn knob.
$10-15

White cake and pie keeper with clamps, chef boy and scottie design.
$15-25

Cake keepers: (left) pink and white with daisy designs, unmarked; (right) aluminum with wood knob, marked "West Bend."
$6-10 (pink); $8-10 (West Bend)

Advertisement for various aluminum kitchenware items by Mirro, from *Look* magazine, November 1955. Notice the increasingly popular copper-tone colored aluminum that was said to give the "glowing warmth of copper."

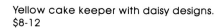
Yellow cake keeper with daisy designs. $8-12

Red cake keeper with flowers painted on side. *Courtesy of Old Town Antique Mall. Portland, Oregon.* $15-20

CANISTERS

Canisters: (left) clover design; (right) blanket flower design.
$4-8 each

Canisters: (left) apple design, Decoware; (center) floral/trellis design, marked "Empeco"; (right) pine cone design, marked "Decoware."
$4-8 each

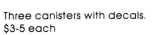
Three canisters with decals.
$3-5 each

Canisters: (left to right) floral design, marked "Ransburg"; fruit design, marked "Decoware"; clover design; petunia design, marked "Decoware."
$4-8 each

Canisters in three sizes, with blueberry design, marked "Decoware," $5-10 depending on size

White canister with stylized farm scene. *Courtesy of Old Town Antique Mall. Portland, Oregon.*
$4-8

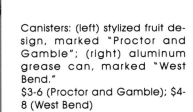

Canisters: (left) stylized fruit design, marked "Proctor and Gamble"; (right) aluminum grease can, marked "West Bend."
$3-6 (Proctor and Gamble); $4-8 (West Bend)

"Cheinco" canister in avocado and green plaid design with white plastic lid, by J. Chein & Co.
$3-6

Canisters in two sizes, from copper set marked "Mirro."
$6-10 depending on size

Four-piece canister set in copper with black plastic base, marked "Beautyware by Lincoln."
$15-20 set

Canisters: (left) large, white with colored aluminum lid and white plastic handle, marked "Ransburg"; (right) cannisters in two sizes from set marked "Decoware."
$4-8

Four-piece canister set, white bodies with copper clad lids, marked "Ransburg." $15-25 set

Flour and sugar canisters from a set, chrome body with copper-clad lids, marked "Lincoln Beautyware." $ 5-8 each

9"-tall pink flour and sugar canisters, marked "Beautyware by Lincoln." $4-8 each

Canisters: (top, left to right) Lincoln Beautyware; tea; Lincoln Beautyware; (bottom, left to right) tea; Pantry Queen; Masterware.
$4-8 each

Grease cans: (left) Heller Hostessware; (right) Heller, metal top.
$5-10 each

Canisters: (left to right) Flour marked "Nasco Italy"; sugar and tea, both marked "Metasco Italy."
$4-8 each

Canisters: (left to right) coffee with plastic lid; covered tin with green Bakelite knob; coffee with plastic knob.
$4-8 (left); $6-10 (center); $4-8 (right)

Four-piece canister set in colored aluminum with black painted lids.
$10-20 set

Four-piece aluminum canister set with vertical lettering.
$15-20 set

Cookie jar marked "West Bend."
$8-12

Four-piece aluminum canister set with black tops, marked "West Bend."
$10-20 set

DISPENSERS

Dispenser for foil, waxed paper, and paper towels, yellow with chef boy and scottie, unmarked.
$10-12

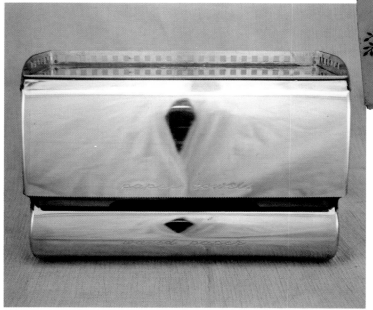

Dispenser for waxed paper and paper towels, unmarked. $4-8.

Dispenser for foil, waxed paper, and paper towels, marked "Sovereign."
$4-8

HOTPADS

Hot Pads: (left) kitchenware illustrations on metal with asbestos backing by Pro-Tex, (right) textured yellow and red on metal with asbestos backing.
$2-6 each

Hot Pads: (left) paper with metal back, advertising Ace Electric Co.; (right) ducks in flight on metal with asbestos backing, by Pro-Tex.
$2-6 each

Hot Pads: two London scenes, from a series on metal with asbestos backing. The back reads "Free with the purchase of eight personal sizes Ivory (soap)."
$2-6 each

Hot Pads: (left) red flowerpots on metal with asbestos backing; (right) Mexican scene on hand-painted and laquered paper with metal backing, unusual.
$2-3 (flowerpots); $6-10 (Mexican scene)

Pro-Tex burner pad.
$2-6

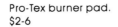

Salt & Pepper Sets

Colored aluminum salt and pepper set with black plastic tops marked "Hawthorn:." $6-12.

Colored aluminum salt and pepper set. $5-10 set

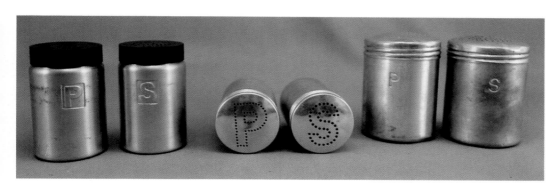

Three marked "Made in Italy." $3-6 each

(From left to right) Aluminum shaker with embossed floral design $4-8.; salt in colored aluminum; $2-4; cleanser can holder (in this case, Old Dutch Cleanser); $10-12; aluminum flour shaker with pink plastic top, marked "Heller Hostessware." $4-8
(From left to right) $4-8; $2-4; $10-12; $4-8

Salt and peppers, all marked "West Bend." $5-8 each

Napkin Holders

Chrome napkin holder with Bakelite base, by the Hero Co.
$8-12

Gold-colored napkin holder.
$2-5

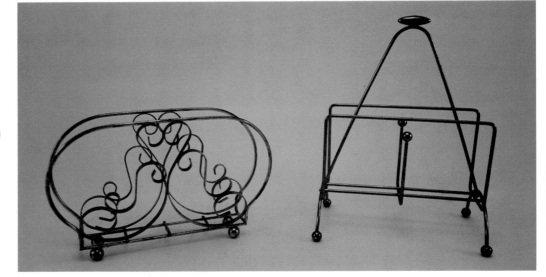

Two napkin holders with ball feet.
$2-6 each

Napkin holders in circular designs.
$2-5 each

RECIPE BOXES

Recipe Boxes: (below) plaid design marked "Ohio Art Co."; (right) fruit design, marked "J. Chein & Co." $3-5 each

Recipe Boxes: (above) food design, marked "Ohio Art Co."; (left) rooster design, marked "Stylecraft of Baltimore." $3-6 each

Recipe Boxes: (left) needlepoint design; (right) herb design, marked "J. Chein & Co." $3-6 each

Recipe Boxes: (left) Pennsylvania Dutch design, marked "Ohio Art Co."; (above) old-fashioned kitchenware designs, marked "Ohio Art Co." $3-6 each

COLORED ALUMINUM

Colored aluminum is anodized aluminum to which colored dyes have been added. Anodizing is an electrical process which coats aluminum pieces with a satin gloss film which bonds with the surface. Anodized aluminum (without colors) appeared in the 1930s on giftwares and serving items.

In 1946 the Aluminum Cooking Utensil Company developed anodized aluminum cookware. By 1950, West Bend had developed a colored anodized aluminum process as well. Other companies produced colored aluminum ware through the 1950s and 1960s, the heyday of its popularity. Colors and shapes vary from company to company. Original colors include blue, silver, green, purple, red, orange, magenta, and gold.

Colored aluminum is another popular and affordable field of collecting right now. Pieces in very good to excellent shape are hard to find. Tumblers and pitchers seem to be the best-remembered items in this field today.

Six colored aluminum tumblers and their stand, marked "Bascal." Courtesy of *Old Town Antique Mall, Portland Oregon.* $25-40 set and stand

Colored aluminum creamer and sugar, marked "Mirro." *Courtesy of Old Town Antique Mall. Portland, Oregon.* $10-15 set

Colored aluminum tumblers in blue and silver, marked "Bombay India." *Courtesy of Old Town Antique Mall. Portland, Oregon.* $4-8 each

Colored aluminum: (left) 5" red bowl; (center) 5"-tall tumbler; (right) 6" blue bowl.
$3-5 (red bowl); $4-6 (tumble); $3-5 (blue bowl)

Colored aluminum: (left) two tumblers in gold and blue, marked "Mirro"; (center) red pitcher, marked "Regal"; (right) two tumblers in red and natural, marked "West Bend."
$3-6 (Mirro); $10-15 (Regal); $3-6 (West Bend)

Colored aluminum items: Butter dish in copper-toned and natural marked West Bend. $3-5; rectangular tray in gold-toned. $2-5; trivet in gold-toned with ivy design. $3-5.

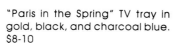

TV Trays

These metal, silkscreen-decorated trays are associated with the 1950s and 1960s, the early days of television. Special versions were made for children.

Each TV tray was attached to a set of rather flimsy folding aluminum legs, and was used to eat a meal while watching TV (most likely a TV dinner.) Some came with smaller fold-down legs for eating in bed.

TV trays have the clamps attached to the back to hold onto the legs.

If you find trays without the clamps, they are probably serving trays. Serving trays are included in this section because of their similarity in appearance and make. Smaller rectangular serving trays from the 1940s with quasi-deco designs are also shown. All above mentioned categories of trays are rarely marked.

"Paris in the Spring" TV tray in gold, black, and charcoal blue. $8-10

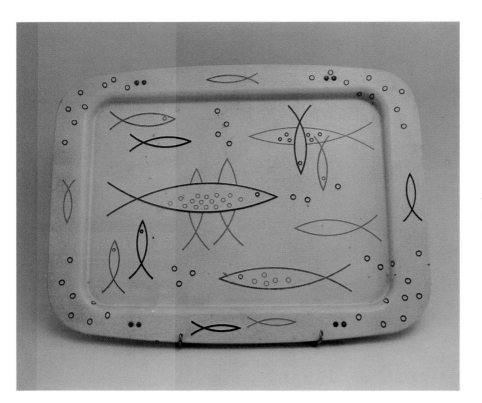

TV tray with stylized fish design. $6-10

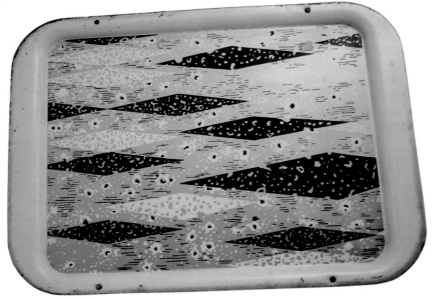

TV tray with abstract design in
black and silver.
$5-10

"Reach for the Rhythm" serving
tray.
$8-10

TV tray with stylized grape design
on dark green.
$4-8

BBQ serving tray. *Courtesy of Palookaville, Portland, Oregon.*
$4-8

Bed tray with stylized floral design in green and white on yellow.
$4-8

Round serving tray with BBQ designs. These trays have been found in two sizes.
$2-5 (small); $6-10 (large)

Serving tray with stylized rooster
design.
$4-8

Serving tray with poodle design.
$5-10

TV tray with anthurium design.
$4-8

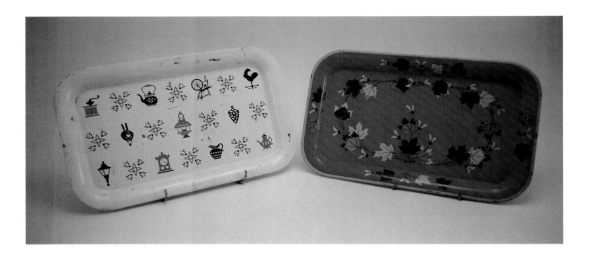

Serving Trays: (left) provincial designs; (right) red with oak leaves.
$4-8 each

Serving tray with poppie design.
Courtesy of Old Town Antique Mall, Portland Oregon.
$3-6

Serving trays: (left) Colonial lady in blue; (right) plate with flowers and grapes.
$4-8 each

Serving tray with fruit design. *Courtesy of Old Town Antique Mall, Portland Oregon.*
$3-6

Green serving tray with parrot design.
$5-10

Black serving tray with gold/white leaf forms and spatters.
$8-10

Utensils & Gadgets

This array of metal kitchenware includes byproducts of technology. Also shown are the uses manufacturers found for new metals, particularly aluminum.

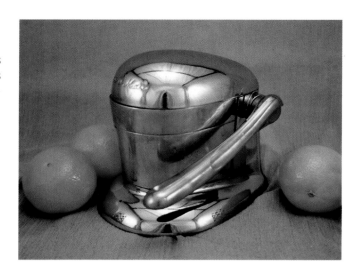

"Juice-O-Mat" juicer by Rival, 1939-1946, des# 1949. $5-15

Juicers: (left) "Juice-O-Mat" in white and chrome by Rival; (right) orange and chrome, marked "Made in Mexico." *Courtesy of Old Town Antique Mall, Portland Oregon.* $10-15 (Juice-O-Mat); $15-25 (orange)

Puree utensil, also known as a Chinoise, marked "Wearever." This item is not complete without the wooden "pestle." *Courtesy of Old Town Antique Mall, Portland Oregon.* $25-30

Table-top manual grinder with Catalin plastic handle, 1932-1959, des# 1959.
$8-12

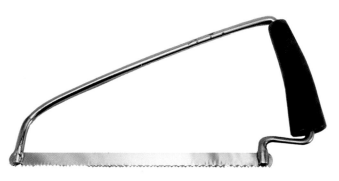

(Top) Meat saw with Catalin handle, rare; (bottom) cake breaker with Catalin handle.
$15-20 (meat saw); $3-6 (cake breaker)

Utensils with Catalin handles: (left to right) two servers, a small frosting knife, a butter knife, and a grapefruit knife.
$4-6 each

Three carving knives with Catalin handles.
$4-6 each

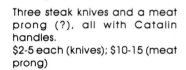
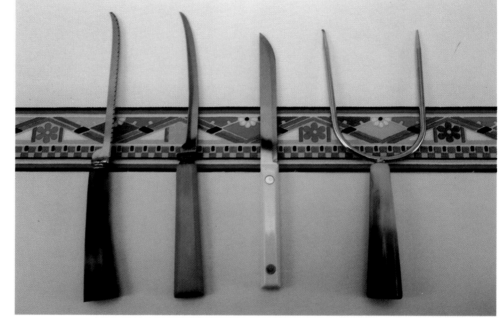

Three steak knives and a meat prong (?), all with Catalin handles.
$2-5 each (knives); $10-15 (meat prong)

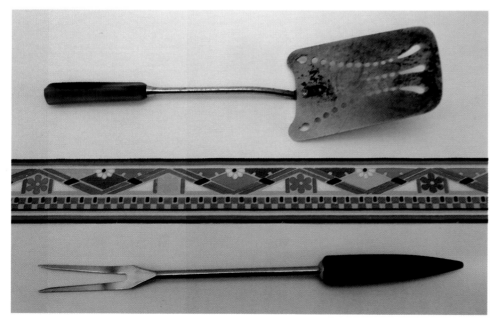

(Top) Spatula, unmarked; (bottom) utility fork, marked "Androck." Both have Catalin handles.
$5-8 (spatula); $6-10 (utility fork)

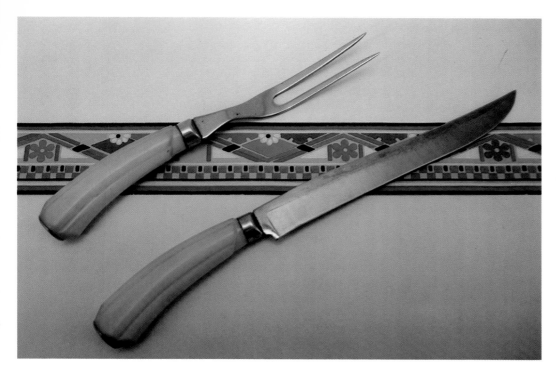

Carving set with Catalin handles, marked "Persona." $15-20 set

Eggbeater, marked "A&J (Ekco Products Co.)." $15-20

(Left) Pastry wheel, marked "Plasmetl"; (center) spatula, unmarked; (right) whip, unmarked. All Catalin handles. $4-6 each

Utensils with Melamine handles in Provincial design II: (left to right) pie server, strainer, kitchenmagig, and spatula. All marked "Flint (Ekco)."
$4-8 each

Three types of spatulas with Melamine handles in Provincial design II.
$4-8 each

Utensils with Melamine handles in Provincial design II: (left to right) masher, utility fork, and utility spoon. All marked "Flint (Ekco)."
$4-8 each

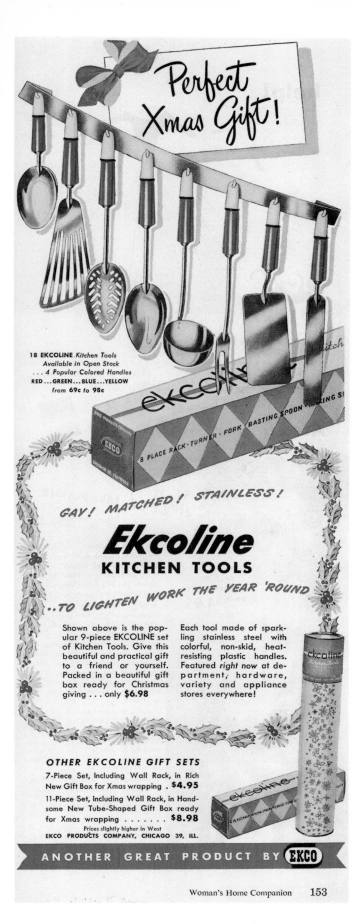

Advertisement showing various utensils by Ekco Products Co., from *Woman's Home Companion*, 1948.

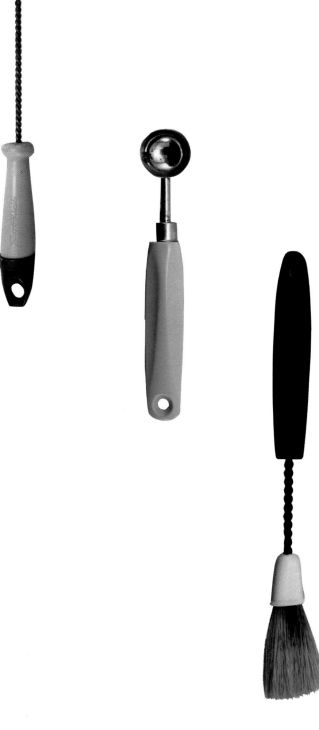

Utensils with miscellaneous plastic handles: (top) pastry brush, marked "Kellogg Quality"; (center) melon scoop; (bottom) pastry brush.
$3-5 each

(Left) "Magic Gadget" utility knife, marked "Regent Sheffield"; (right) frosting spatula, marked "A&J."
$3-6 each

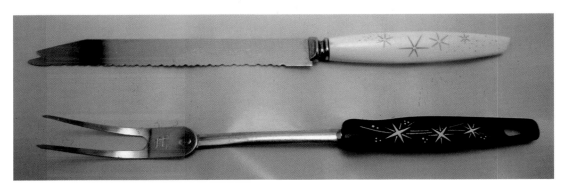

(Top) Bread knife, marked "Sheffield"; (right) utility fork, marked "Ekco."
$4-6 each

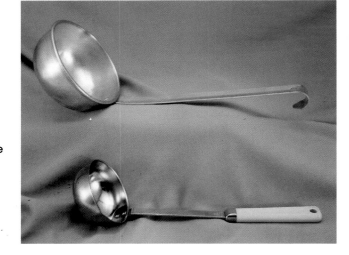

Aluminum and stainless steel ladles, one with pink plastic handle marked "Maid of Honor."
$3-6 each

Pot drainer with turquoise wooden handle, marked "Foley," 1950. *Courtesy of Old Town Antique Mall. Portland, Oregon.*
$4-6

Strainers with wood handles.
$3-6 each

Strainers with wood handles.
$2-4 each

(Top) Strainer; (bottom) whip marked "Batter Beater A&J."
$6-10

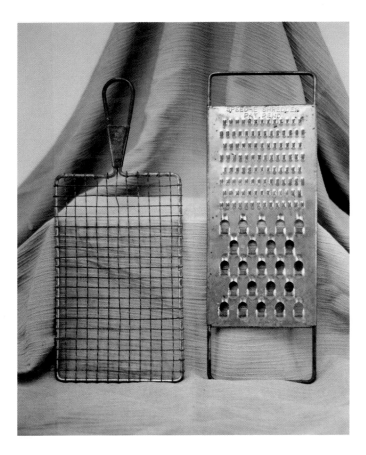

Graters: (left) marked "ACME, the only genuine safety grater";
(right) unmarked.
$4-8 each

Graters: (left) marked "All in One"; (left) marked "Speed-E shred-
der."
$4-8 each

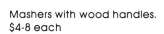

Mashers with wood handles.
$4-8 each

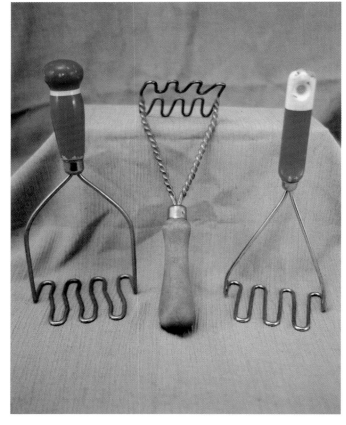

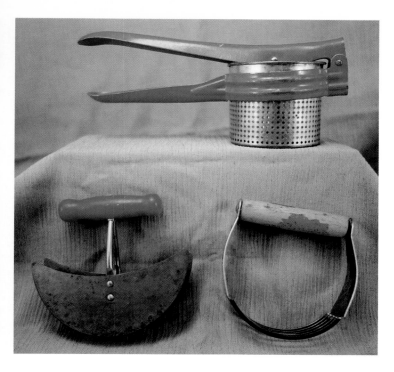

(Top) Potato masher; (bottom left) chopper marked "ACME"; (bottom right) dough blender marked "Ekco."
$8-12 (potato masher); $4-8 each (chopper and blender)

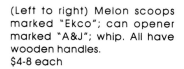

(Left to right) Melon scoops marked "Ekco"; can opener marked "A&J"; whip. All have wooden handles.
$4-8 each

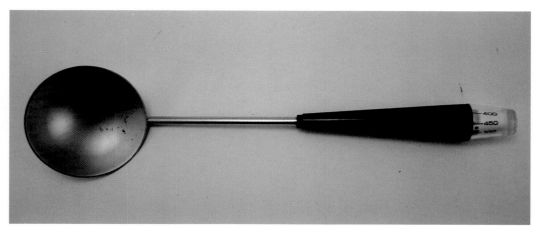

"Tempstir," a spoon/thermometer combination. New in 1964, the Tempstir had a see-through window at the end of the handle, which housed the thermometer dial. It originally sold for $4.95.
$10-15

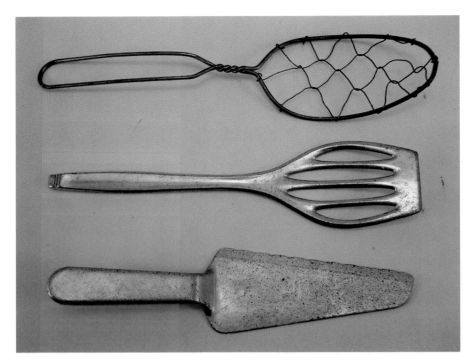

Two slotted spoons and a cake knife.
$4-8

Aluminum juicer marked Foley with 1950 Patent #; whisk with nylon resin handle. The whisk design here has changed very little since its introduction almost a century ago. The handle, however, has gone through many changes in materials.
$3-5 each.

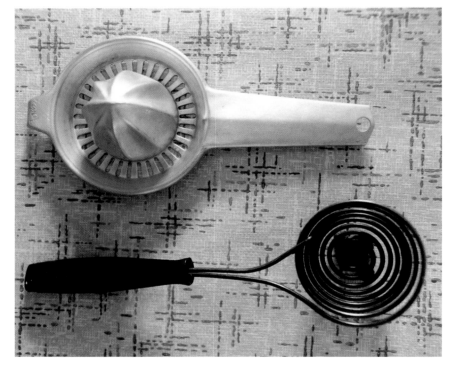

(Left to right) Fish scaler marked "Chief"; peeler and bean frencher marked "Ekco," 1940; nutmeg grater marked "M.E. Heuck Co.," 1938.
$4-6 each

Food decorator marked "Quikut Division Scott & Fetzer Co."; juice extractor marked "Safta Westamark Made in W. Germany"; krinkle cutter.
$2-3 (decorator and extractor); $4-6 (krinkle cutter)

Strawberry huller; "Mendets" pot menders.
$5-8 each

Tongs made of anodized aluminum, marked "Magic Hostess."
$2-6

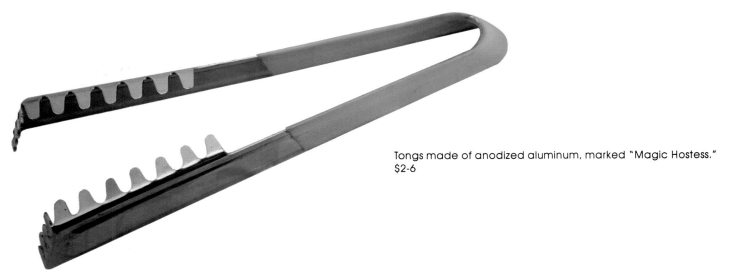

(Left to right) Kitchenmajig, marked "A&J"; ladle marked "A&J"; spoon marked "A&J"; slicer marked "Ekco." All with wooden handles.
$4-8 each

Two spatulas with wooden handles, marked "Ekco" and "Chief."
$4-8 each

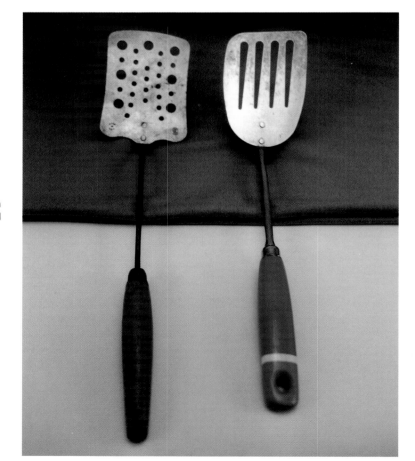

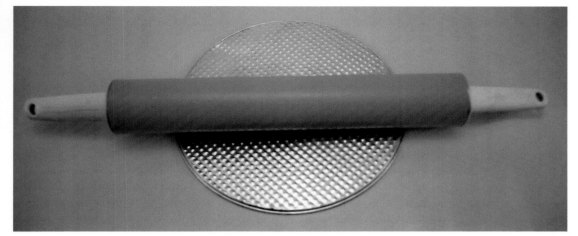

Rolling pin in pink and white.
$4-8

Sifters: (left) white with stylized wheat, unmarked; (right) white with blue and black designs, marked "Androck."
$5-10 each

your best buy...

MIRRO
THE FINEST ALUMINUM

Cooky, Pastry Press and Decorator Set

all for only $3.95
(West, 4.35)

Set includes Cooky and Pastry Press with copper-tone trim, 12 cooky forming plates, 3 pastry tips, plus Decorator, with 6 design tips, step-by-step directions and tested recipes, complete.

gorgeous desserts, easy as pie!

Each quick quarter-turn of the handle of the new MIRRO Press creates a new cooky, in the interesting shape you select. And the generous barrel of the press holds enough dough, at one filling, for five dozen cookies! With the pastry tips you turn out eclairs, cream puffs, ladyfingers, or meringues, all with the same ease, the same professional look.

Then, with the MIRRO Decorator, you quickly duplicate the rosettes, ribbons, petals and flowers of the practiced pastry chef, giving cookies and cakes the extra loveliness that makes them truly party-pretty. Get MIRRO at department, hardware and home furnishing stores, wherever dealers sell the finest aluminum.

ALUMINUM GOODS MANUFACTURING CO., MANITOWOC, WISCONSIN
World's Largest Manufacturer of Aluminum Cooking Utensils

MIRRO	14 x 10",	$1.00 (West 1.10)
COOKY	15½ x 12",	$1.15 (West 1.25)
SHEETS	17 x 14",	$1.50 (West 1.65)

Cookie cutters: (left to right) red wooden knob; green wooden knob; green metal knob. *Courtesy of Old Town Antique Mall, Portland Oregon.*
$3-5

Advertisement showing Cooky Press and Decorator by Mirro, from *Better Homes & Gardens,* December 1956.

Cooky press marked "Mirro";
cake decorator marked "Mirro."
$10-15 each

Cookie gun and pastry decorator marked "Wearever." *Courtesy
of Palookaville, Portland, Oregon.*
$4-8

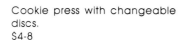

Cookie press with changeable
discs.
$4-8

Cookie press with 11 changeable discs and a pastry nozzle in aluminum. 1938 Patent #. $6-8

Foley sifter; Foley aluminum funnel; combination spatula/bottle opener advertising "Albers Flapjack Flour"; aluminum measuring cup.
$3-6 (sifter); $2-4 (funnel); $8-12 (spatula); $2-4 (measuring cup)

Small loaf pan by Emco. The quilted version of this OVENEX line is more popular with collectors than the plain lines.
$3-5

Measuring pitcher marked "Royal"; two funnels.
$4-8 (pitcher); $3-6 each (funnels)

(Left) Measuring set, aluminum; candy thermometer, in box with instructions.
$2-4 (measuring set); $8-12 (thermometer)

Scoops: (top to bottom) colored aluminum (1 tsp.); Caswell coffee; colored aluminum (1/3 cup).
$2-3 (1 tsp.); $5-10 (coffee); $3-5 (1/3 cup)

Scoops: (left to right) colored aluminum with clad-bottom look;
nested cups in two sizes, from a measuring set; (in back) Colored
aluminum hot pad.
$1-2 (cups); $3-5 (hot pad)

Measures: colored aluminum set; 1/2 cup; 1/3 cup; spoon set.
$3-6 (colored alum. set); $2-8 each (spoons)

Advertisement showing "Magic Touch" ice cube trays by Inland Mfg. Co., from *Better Homes & Gardens*, July 1948.

Ice cube tray: Holder in blue colored aluminum; divider in natural aluminum reads "Magic Touch SPIL-GARD". $1-3.

"Quickube" double ice cube tray, marked "Frigidaire." $1-3 each

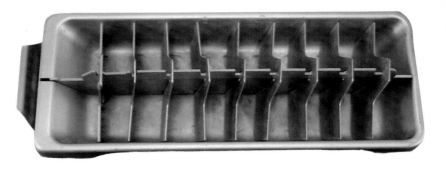

Ice cube trays by Frigidaire.
$1-3 each

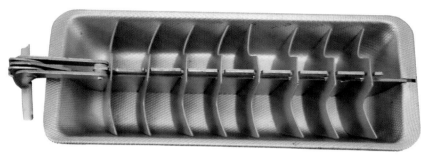

Ice cube trays: (top) unmarked;
(bottom) Philco.
$1-3 each

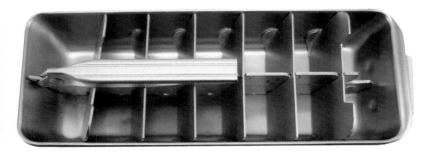

Ice cube trays: (top) colored
aluminum; (bottom) Montgomery Wards.
$1-3

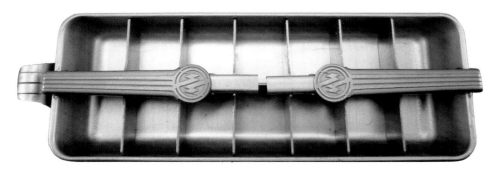

"Roaster-Broiler-Server" broiler pan by West Bend, with duck and cattail design, 1942-1950, des# 1947.
$5-10

"Serv-Hot Grill" broiler pan by George D. Roper Corp., 1947.
$3-5

Pie plates.
$3-6 each

Dust pans: (left) floral design, "JV
Reed"; (right) provincial design,
"JV Reed."
$2-4 each

Dust pans: (left) floral design,
marked; fruit design.
$2-4 each

Match holders, wall type.
$4-8 each

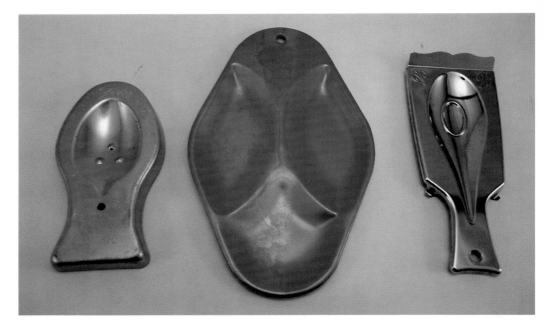

Spoon rests: (left to right) "Tidy Spoon"; red colored aluminum; stainless steel.
$2-3 each

Wall-hanging planters in musical motifs.
$5-8 each

Wall hangers: gay '90s couple.
$4-8 set

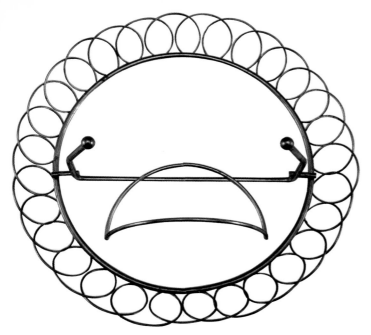

Wall-hanging planter.
$5-8

Luau torches, aluminum, in box,
marked "Noma Patio Products."
$4-8

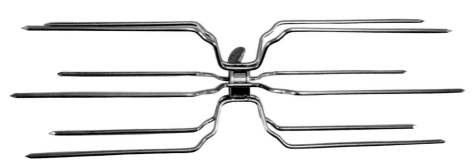

Hot dog spit rotator, marked
"Ekco."
$2-5

Cocktail shaker in aluminum; thermos by Aladdin; Bar Aid
drink guide. The thermos must have all four parts to be
complete — the body, the lining, the top which doubles
as a cup, and the plug or opening.
$2-5 (shaker, Bar Aid); $10-12 (thermos)

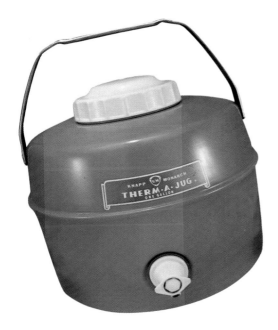

"Therm-A-Jug" insulated cooler by Knapp Monarch, in
pink.
$4-8

Sink drainer in aluminum; table crumbsweeper with
Catalin handle; Mirromatic timer.
$1-2 (drainer); $6-10 (crumbsweeper); $4-6 (timer)

Burner pad with pierced metal body and adjustable handle, by Pro Tex.
$2-4

Iron rests.
$2-4 each

"Cadie" pressing cloth by Cadie Chemical Prod. Inc.
$4-8.

ADVERTISEMENTS

Advertising is a huge collectible field unto itself, but here we will restrict ourselves mainly to magazine advertisements. Way back when, collectible dealers found that an old magazine was worth more page by page than as a whole. While this theory sounds somewhat unscrupulous, I am sure many beautiful pages were saved from partly ruined magazines that would have gone into the trash. Regardless of motives, people seem to love old advertisements. At any given collector's show, there will be a paper booth with ads tucked away with old crate labels and post cards. Don't pass up old magazines if you come upon them at a sale or shop. Women's magazines and household magazines are likely to contain the most kitchen- and appliance-oriented ads.

Expect to pay anywhere from $5-25 for old magazines, with most costing less than $10. Old ads, neatly cut from magazines, shrink-wrapped on board, should run in the $10-20 range, depending on condition, color vs. black and white, etc.

Advertisement endorsing Brillo Soap Pads, from *Good Housekeeping*, March 1952.

Cleaners: (left) ZUD, from Rustain Products; (center) Never-Dull wadding polish by the George Basch Co.; (right) NEW Old Dutch Cleanser, from the Cudahy Packing Co., 1953.
$3-6 each

Wall mounted dispenser for powdered Borax in porcelain enamel with natural steel parts. Lettering is screen-printed on. $10-20.

"Magic-Foil" aluminum wrap. $3-5

Disposable aluminum fry pans in bag, from the E-Z Por Corp. $2-3

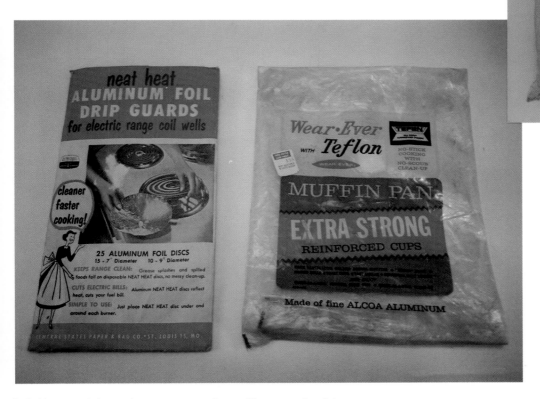

Foil drip guards in package; wrapper for muffin pan advertising Teflon. $2-3 (guards); $1-2 (wrapper)

Advertisement promoting the use of aluminum, from *Better Homes & Gardens,* July 1948.

Advertisement extolling the virtues of S.O.S. Magic Soap Pads, from *Woman's Home Companion,* November 1948.

Advertisement for S.O.S. Magic Scouring Pads, from *Good Housekeeping,* May 1938. "A dip, a rub, a rinse —Aluminum shines like new."

Advertisement showing various aluminum products using ALCOA aluminum, from *Better Homes & Gardens,* December 1953. I love the idea of an aluminum Christmas!

Advertisement promoting electrical use in the home, from *Look,* May 1957.

Advertisement for the Servel "Electric Wonderbar," from *Better Homes & Gardens,* October 1952. I guess the next best thing to finding one of these obscure electric items would be owning the ad. Where did these things go?

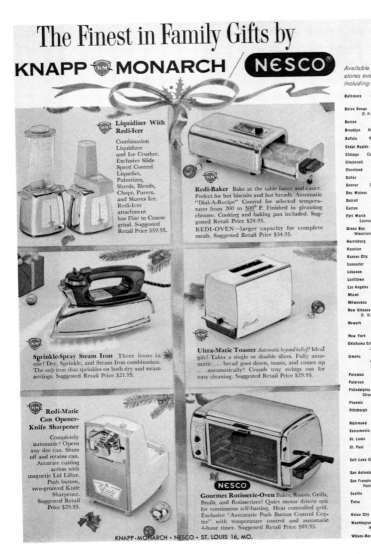

Advertisement featuring various Knapp Monarch / NESCO appliances, from *House Beautiful*, 1960.

Advertisement promoting a Hotpoint All-Electric Kitchen by General Electric, from *Good Housekeeping*, June 1951. This ad contains all the catchphrases found in electrical ads of the era: "electric," "automatic," "work-saving," and "push button."

Advertisement featuring the "Control Master" by Presto, from *Better Homes & Gardens*, December 1956. Presto was one of the early companies to feature a master control unit on the cord that was detachable and could be plugged into the whole line of the company's appliances.

Advertisement for GE appliances featuring a rotisserie, from *The Saturday Evening Post*, October 1958.

Advertisement showing the NuTone Built-in Food Center, from *House & Garden*, November 1956. A novel and intriguing idea that never took off.

Advertisement promoting the use of stainless steel by United States Steel, from *Better Homes & Gardens*, 1948. U.S. Steel employed noted book illustrator Keith Ward to illustrate a series of ads pushing the advantages of stainless steel in the kitchen.

TO WISH HER THE BEST GIVE HER THE BEST...

TOASTMASTER

CHRISTMAS... First something frilly and feminine, because she's so lovely. And then one of these helping hands from Toastmaster, to show her she's a wonderful homemaker...

Any of these Toastmaster Automatic Appliances will do the trick. All of them are made with the same care and precision... each of them will make her days more pleasant for years to come. And isn't that as it should be?

A   TOASTMASTER POWERMATIC TOASTER
Completely automatic—you don't even press a lever! Lowers the bread, toasts it, serves it up high. Perfect for muffins, frozen waffles and pancakes, too. $28.50. 3-slice, $39.50.

B   NEW TOASTMASTER AUTOMATIC COFFEE MAKER
Makes finer-flavored coffee—3 cups or 10—at the rate of a cup a minute! Exclusive "Flavor Dome" top, two heating elements bring out all the flavor. Completely automatic. $29.95.

C   NEW TOASTMASTER STEAM AND DRY IRON
Two irons in one! Steam or dry at a touch of the dial! Steady steam, no sputtering—presses without damp cloth, irons most fabrics without sprinkling. Fabric Selector Dial. $16.95.

D   NEW TOASTMASTER AUTOMATIC TOASTER
Smart new styling... sleek low black and gold handles! Perfect toast every time. Toast Control Dial, hinged crumb tray. $18.95. Others from $15.95 to $23.00.

E   NEW TOASTMASTER AUTOMATIC FRY PAN
Cooks everything from bacon to cake... fries, bakes, roasts, stews! Controls temperatures automatically. Immersible. 11″, $19.95; 12″, $24.95. Matching vented covers, $3.25, $4.25.

more family friends....from **TOASTMASTER**   McGRAW EDISON   TOASTMASTER DIVISION McGRAW-EDISON COMPANY

"TOASTMASTER" is a registered trademark of McGraw-Edison Company, Elgin, Ill., and Oakville, Ont. ©1957

Advertisement for various Toastmaster appliances by McGraw Edison, from *Better Homes & Gardens,* December 1957.

Recipe Booklets

Recipe booklets (also called cookbook pamphlets) are different from regular cookbooks. They are usually soft-backed, measure about 8 x 10 inches or less, and have fewer than 50 pages. All the recipe booklets shown here were published by appliance makers, and were usually acquired by sending away to the manufacturer. These recipe booklets promoted the appliances through exuberant copy, luscious photographs, and delectable recipes.

Cookbook collectors have discovered these paperbacked gems in recent years and have slowly added them to their collections. Nonetheless, these booklets are still easy to find, though pre-World War II items might be scarcer and pricey. Search for the books that go with your appliances or start a collection of books by themselves! They have great pictures and wonderful recipes. In addition, some booklets show other products offered by the company. This has been extremely helpful to me (and maybe to you, too).

Recipe booklets sell for anywhere from a few dollars up to $20 for older & rarer items.

Dominion Grid-O-Matic Automatic Table Cooker, Dominion Electric Corporation, brochure type, 1950s.

A Wealth of Wonderful Recipes, Country Inn Cookware, West Bend Company, 37 pgs, 1969.

New Westinghouse Cook-N-Fryer, Westinghouse Corporation, 31 pgs, circa early 1950s.

Kitchen Tested Recipes, Sunbeam Mixmaster, Sunbeam Corporation, 36 pgs, circa 1940.

340 Recipes for the new Waring Blendor, Waring Products Corporation, 64 pgs, 1947.

Teflon Coated Automatic Electric Skillet, Recipes and Instructions, Westbend Corporation, brochure type, circa 1964.

Unusual Old World and American Recipes, Nordic Ware, Northland, Aluminum Prods, Inc., 48 pgs, circa early 1960s.

Westinghouse Roaster Oven and Infra-Red Broiler Grid, Westinghouse Electric Corporation, 34 pgs, circa 1950.

Electric Mix Treasures, Dormeyer Meal-Maker, Dormeyer Corporation, 36 pgs, 1949

Kenmore Automatic Grill-Waffler, Sears, Roebuck & Company, 22 pgs, 1950s.

Pressure Sauce Pan, General Electric, 12 pgs, early 1950s.

Roto-Broil '400' King Size, Roto-Broil Corporation of America, 16 pgs, late 1950s.

Instructions and Tested Recipes, Food Mixer & Mixguide, Hamilton Beach, 52 pgs, circa 1948.

How to get the Most out of Your Sunbeam Mixmaster, Sunbeam Corporation, 44 pgs, 1948.

Waring Blendor Cook Book, Waring Products Corporation, 66 pgs, 1955.

Recipes and Instruction, Presto Dixie-Fryer, National Pressure Cooker Company, 42 pgs, 1950.

GE Automatic Skillet, General Electric, 36 pgs, late 1950s.

Instructions and Recipes, Wear-Ever Salad Maker, Aluminum Cooking Utensil Company, 18 pgs, 1955.

Presto Cooker Recipe Book, National Pressure Cooker Company, 130 pgs, 1947.

Cook Master Heat Control, Landers of Arkansas, 24 pgs, 1957.

Electric Cookery, Montgomery Wards, 50 pgs, 1948.

101 Refrigerator Helps, Frigidaire Division, General Motors, 34 pgs, 1944.

Around the World Cook Book, Kalamazoo Stove & Furnace Company, 50 pgs, 1951.

Recipes and Instructions, Ovenette, West Bend Aluminum Company, 16 pgs, 1940s.

Tasty Recipes, Oster Mixers, John Oster Manufacturing Company 34 pgs, 1946.

Cook-a-matic Waffle-Grill, Universal, 24 pgs, 1948.

Old-Fashioned Bean Pot Cookery, West Bend Aluminum Company, 16 pgs, 1955.

Presto Vertical Broiler, National Presto Industries, Inc., 22 pgs, 1960s.

Electric Cooking with your Kenmore Range, Sears & Roebuck, 34 pgs, 1956.

Cutco Cook Book (World's Finest Cutlery!), Wear-Ever Aluminum Company, 130 pgs, 1961. Great photos of their complete line.

The Use and Care of Miracle Maid Cook-Ware, Advance Aluminum Castings Corporation, 32 pgs, 1947.

New Exciting! Casual Cooking, Reynolds Metals Company, 16 pgs. 1954.

Revere's Guide to Better Cooking, Revere Copper and Brass Inc., 32 pgs, 1941.

Frozen Food Cook Book, Amana Refrigeration Inc., 66 pgs, 1953

Coldspot Freezers, Sears, Roebuck, & Company, 38 pgs, 1950.

Recipe Booklet from Coldspot Freezers, 1951.

Recipe Booklet from Miracle Maid Cookware, 1947.

Recipe Booklet from Revere, 1941.

Recipe Booklet from Sunbeam Mixmaster, 1948.

Recipe Booklet from Presto Dixie Fryer, 1950.

Recipe Booklet from Universal Waffle/Grill, 1948.

Serving Pieces, Holders, and Warmers

This section covers a variety of categories: serving pieces, holders for tumblers, holders for casseroles, and warmers. A warmer might be described as any holder used to hold a non-electric appliance, cookware item, or casserole piece, usually with a smaller holder attached underneath which held a candle or sterno can to keep the contents of the item warm. Derived from the chafing dish, warmers began as more decorative pieces and ended in the 1960s as nondescript, skeletal, wrought iron affairs.

Advertisement showing various serving pieces, from the "Kensington" line by the Aluminum Cooking Utensil Co., from *House & Garden*, November 1956.

Copper and brass serving tray with Bakelite handle, unmarked. Unusual piece. $15-20

(Left) "Penguin" Cold Hot Server, by West Bend, 1945 des# 1942; (right) ice bucket, spun and painted aluminum, unmarked. $15-30 (Penguin); $8-10 (ice bucket)

Cocktail shaker and ice bucket, marked "Leumas-Handcrafted giftware." *Courtesy of Palookaville, Portland, Oregon.* $10-15 set

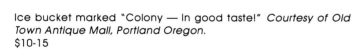

Ice bucket marked "Colony — In good taste!" *Courtesy of Old Town Antique Mall, Portland Oregon.* $10-15

Spun aluminum serving bowl with wood base. $6-10

Salad fork and spoon, stainless steel with black plastic handles.
$5-10 set

Chrome over aluminum serving tray, leaf shape, unmarked.
$4-8

Coasters: floral and duck designs.
$4-8 each

Coasters: copper with wildlife scenes.
$6-8 each.

Coasters: (left) Stanhome; (right) Reynolds Aluminum logo. $4-8 each

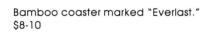

Bamboo coaster marked "Everlast." $8-10

Trivets: (left) 8" pierced design, expands to hold larger pieces; (right) 6" chrome marked "Manning Bowman." $4-8 each

Aluminum serving tray, "Company for Supper" design, acrylic handles, unmarked.
$5-10

Serving oven or bun warmer by Mirro in spun aluminum with bamboo handle and wood knob.
.$8-12.

Serving ovens or bun warmers by West Bend: (left) aluminum; (right) avocado-colored aluminum. There is a trivet which fits into this type of warmer and is not complete without it.
$6-12 (left); $4-6 (right)

Round serving tray in black with bridal theme in white and pink. $4-8. (place after 16/01)

Metal bowl in flying saucer shape with pink interior. Unusual piece.
$15-30

Serving tray made of brass-colored pierced metal.
$5-8

Serving tray made of brass-colored pierced metal.
$5-8

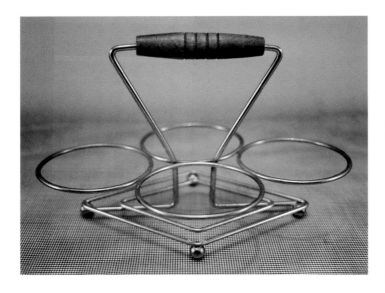

Condiment holder, four sections with wooden handle.
$3-5

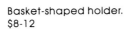

Basket-shaped holder.
$8-12

A holder — though for what I'm not sure.
$4-6

Plant or drink holder; spice jar holder; planter and bill holder.
$3-6 each

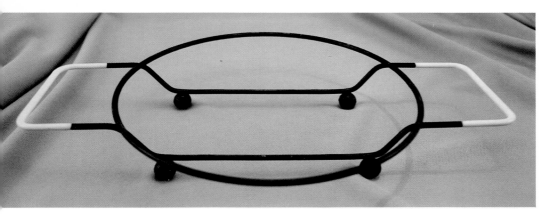

Casserole holder in wrought iron with rubber handles.
$2-5

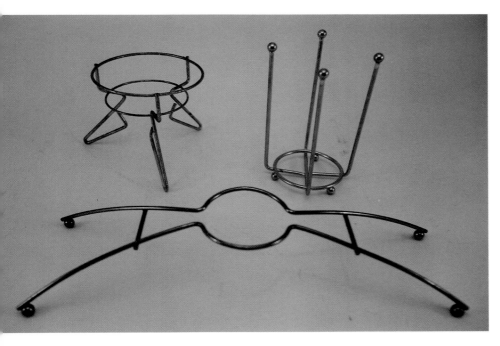

Three holders, two with ball feet.
$3-5

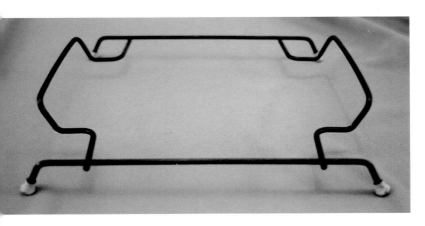

Casserole holder in wrought iron.
$2-5

Casserole holders in chrome with Catalin handles, 1930s.
$5-10

Casserole holder with white plastic handles.
$2-3

Casserole holder, possibly institutional ware.
$2-3

Casserole holder made of hammered copper, expands to hold bigger casseroles.
$5-10

Holder for six tumblers.
$4-6

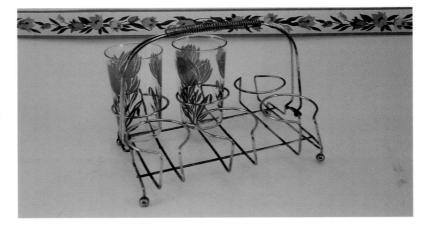

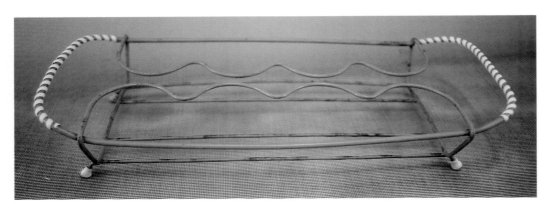

Holder for eight tumblers.
$4-6

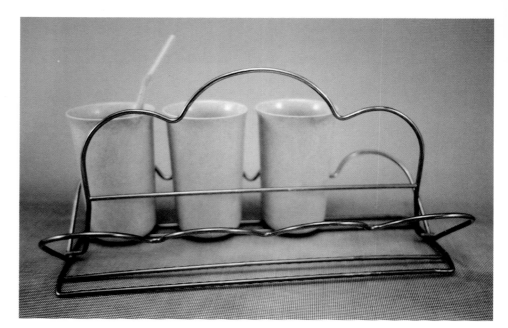

Holder for eight tumblers.
$4-6

Holder for eight tumblers, with wooden handle.
$4-8

Holder with six glasses and four bowls. *Courtesy of Old Town Antique Mall, Portland Oregon.* $40-50 complete set

Copper warmer with white plastic woven handles.
$5-10

Warmers: (left) pierced metal; (right) metal with insect decorated ceramic insert.
$3-5 (pierced); $8-12 (insect)

Two warmers in black. *Courtesy of Urban Edge, Portland, Oregon.*
$4-6

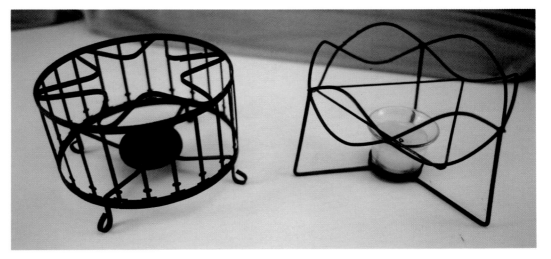

Two warmers in black. *Courtesy of Urban Edge, Portland, Oregon.*
$4-6

Aluminum serving tray in a Masonic design, marked "Portland, Oregon."
$10-15

Hammered aluminum serving pieces: a covered bowl marked "Farberware"; a basket-shaped dish with handle, marked "Everlast."
$6-10 (covered bowl); $4-8 (dish)

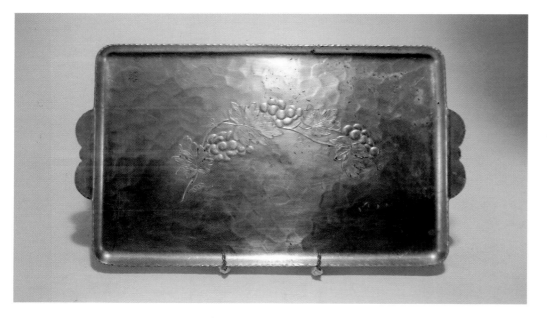

Hammered aluminum tray with grape design, marked "Everlast." *Courtesy of Earl Rich, Portland Oregon.*
$4-8

Hammered aluminum serving tray in a rose design, marked "Continental." *Tray courtesy of David King, Portland Oregon.* $25-35

Hammered aluminum serving tray in a grape design, marked "Everlast." *Tray courtesy of Earl Rich, Portland Oregon.* $10-15

Hammered aluminum serving tray in an apple design, marked "Everlast." *Tray courtesy of Earl Rich, Portland, Oregon.* $10-15

139

Hammered aluminum serving bowls: (left) acorn design, marked "Continental"; (right) floral design, marked "Everlast." *Bowls courtesy of Earl Rich, Portland, Oregon.*
$10-20 (acorn); $10-15 (floral)

Hammered aluminum serving pieces: (left) casserole holder, unmarked; (right) covered bowl, unmarked. *Casserole holder courtesy of Earl Rich, Portland, Oregon.*
$6-10 (casserole holder); $8-12 (covered bowl)

Hammered aluminum leaf-shaped serving dish marked BW Buenilum.
$8-12.

Hammered aluminum serving pieces: butter dish with leaf design, marked "Farberware"; tray with floral design, unmarked. *Butter dish courtesy of Earl Rich, Portland, Oregon.*
$6-10 (butter dish); $4-8 (tray)

Hammered aluminum serving tray in a floral design, marked "National Silver." $10-15

Hammered aluminum serving plate in a floral design, marked "Everlast." $8-12

POTS 'N' PANS

The history of metal cooking utensils in America is as old as the country itself. The original metals were iron and tin. The first cast iron pots were produced by the Saugus Iron Works around 1640 in Massachusetts. The first tinware made in America was produced in 1720 in Connecticut, though tinplate had been imported from England for many years. The arrival of porcelain enameling (see Enamel) in the 1870s launched a great new era for the nation's cookware industry. The first porcelain enamel cooking utensils to be manufactured in the U.S. was by J. Vollrath in Wisconsin. Next came aluminum, once a prohibitively expensive metal. By 1890, the first stamped and cast aluminum cookware was made by the Aluminum Company of America (ALCOA). Aluminum (along with enamelware and cast iron) dominated the cookware scene until the 1930s, when stainless steel made inroads. In 1935 the first stainless-clad carbon steel core cookware for home use appeared. The next twenty-five years saw a series of upgrades and combinations of metals used in producing more efficient cookware: Revere Ware, introduced in 1937, the first copper-clad bottom stainless steel cookware; aluminum clad bottom stainless steel utensils by Farber, using their special "Farberware" process, in 1949; stainless-clad carbon steel core cookware made by Carrollton, Polar and Nesco, in 1950; porcelain enamel aluminumware developed and first offered to the public by Club Aluminum Products, 1953; and the first stainless steel clad aluminum, offered by the West Bend and Regal Ware companies, in 1960.

ENAMEL
(ALSO CALLED PORCELAIN ENAMEL)

Enamel is a glasslike substance used to form a smooth, glossy surface on metal. It is mainly composed of powdered lead-soda glass or lead-potash glass. Metallic oxides are added to produce different colors. It provides a tough protective surface for kitchen appliances, pots, pans, and cookware, which have come to be called "enamelware" by collectors. Many early twentieth-century kitchen items were enameled, including utensils, countertops, canisters, and bread boxes.

The word enamel also refers to enamel paint, which forms a hard, glossy surface when dried. Painting something with enamel paint is not the same as enamelware.

Care and Cleaning: Enamel is usually applied over cast iron, tin, or stainless steel/aluminum mixtures. Enamelware scratches and edges chip. Metal utensils used on enameled cookware will rub or chip off the insides over a period of time, exposing the metal underneath. Exposed cast iron may rust and discolor foods. Enamelware is easy to clean. Soap and water or an all purpose cleaner will do the job. A #0000 steel wool pad will help greatly with baked-on grease.

Advertisement showing enamel paint — which is not the same as porcelain enamel — from *Good Housekeeping*, 1956.

Advertisement extolling the virtues of Enameledware porcelain on steel, from *Better Homes & Gardens*, July 1948.

Enamelware: (left) saucepan in white with red; (center) double boiler in white with red; (right) saucepan in white with black. $4-6 each (saucepans); $5-10 (double boiler)

Enamelware kettle in white with red. $10-25

Enamelware strainer in white and blue. *Courtesy of Old Town Antique Mall, Portland Oregon.* $20-25

Large enamelware pan with blue swirl outside. *Courtesy of Old Town Antique Mall, Portland Oregon.* $30-35

Enamelware: 6" plate and cup in white with blue. *Courtesy of Old Town Antique Mall, Portland Oregon.*
$2-4 each

Enamelware coffee pot in dark blue with white spatters. *Courtesy the collection of David Kohl, Portland Oregon.*
$15-20

GRANITEWARE

Graniteware is really one type of Enamelware. Most enamelware, particularly the older pieces, is referred to as Graniteware. Appearing in the years after the Civil War, Graniteware was the first commercial cookware to be made with enamel. Until this time iron and tin were the main materials used for cookware. The early graniteware was colored a now-familiar mottled gray which resembled granite, hence the name. By World War I, there were over eighty companies producing graniteware, and by the 1920s Graniteware was being produced in various patterns and colors. The patterns (names like Spattered, Mottled, Feathered, Speckled, and Swirl speak for themselves) were created by combining white with either blue, teal green, green, brown, or red. The idea of brightly colored utilitarian items was an instant success. Almost ever conceivable kitchen implement or utilitarian household item was manufactured in graniteware. Graniteware's brief success started to fade as interest in aluminum cookware increased, along with the introduction of Pyrex in the 1920s.

Graniteware was still being made in the 1950s, but was generally referred to as Enameled Ware. Most pieces were much lighter, and were enameled white with either red, deep blue, or black trim. Other color combinations include cream with green trim and light brown with black. Plates, cups, strainers, saucepans, kettles, and leftover dishes were some of the many enameled items offered.

Large graniteware coffee pot. *Courtesy of Old Town Antique Mall, Portland Oregon.*
$35-50

Graniteware: (left) muffin tin; (right) funnel. *Courtesy of Old Town Antique Mall, Portland Oregon.*
$10-15 (muffin tin); $15-30 (funnel)

Deep fryer insert.
$2-4

Steamer insert.
$3-5

Two sizes of double boilers, both by Comet, "the popular aluminum."
$6-8 (small); $8-12 (large)

Skillets: (left) yellow enameled marked "Belgium"; (right) marked Wearever, with bottom reading "for cleaning, use SOS scouring pads."
$3-6 each

Porcelain enamel cast iron oval baker in turquoise, marked "Made in France." May be newer.
$8-12

Advertisement featuring the "Thermo Chef" skillet by Micro-Moisture Controls Inc., from *Good Housekeeping,* December 1956.

Saucepan with Bakelite handle, marked "Made in Italy"; "Muffinaire" muffin pan by United Aircraft Products Inc., 1935. $3-5 (saucepan); $4-8 (muffin pan)

Saucepans: (left) 5", marked "Wearever"; (right) 7", marked "Worthmore Aluminum." $3-5 each

Advertisement showing "Magnalite" saucepans in cast aluminum by Wagner, from *McCall's* magazine, November 1955.

Sectional skillet marked "The Everedy Co.," unusual.
$4-8

Square frying pan marked "Mirro," unusual.
$4-8

Three cast aluminum covered saucepans, marked "Wagner Ware 'Magnalite'."
$10-20 each

"BaconEgger" by Everedy Co. Both pieces must be together to be complete.
$10-20

147

Advertisement showing Club Aluminum Waterless Cooker, from *Good Housekeeping,* November 1954.

Waterless cooker marked "Lifetime," precursor to pressure cookers.
$5-10

Pressure Cooker: Steel or iron with steel coating made by the National Pressure Cooker Company later called PRESTO.
$10-25.

148

Coffee Pots

"Kwik Drip Coffee Maker" by West Bend, aluminum, holds 18 cups, three-piece large pot with Bakelite handle and knob. $10-20

Aluminum coffee pot in old-fashioned urn shape. *Courtesy the collection of David Kohl, Portland, Oregon.* $15-20

Coffee pot with upsweeping upside-down handle, by Wearever. *Courtesy the collection of David Kohl, Portland, Oregon.* $10-20

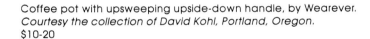

(Left) "Comet " and (right) "Wear-Ever" coffee pots. *Courtesy the collection of David Kohl, Portland,Oregon.* $10-20 each

Coffee pots: (left) "Flavo-Drip" Deluxe aluminum by West Bend, des# 1940; (right) Wear Ever Aluminum, des# 1935. *Both pieces courtesy the collection of David Kohl, Portland, Oregon.* $10-20 each

Pots and Pans: Teapot marked "Universal Tea Ball - Tea Pot" by Landers, Frary & Clark. Printed on the tea ball is "Pat Nov 7, 1907, Brit. Pat. 1909 and a Russian Pat 1911!! Unusual. $10-20.

Coffee pots: (left) marked "Duralux"; (right) marked "ABCO". *Both pieces courtesy the collection of David Kohl, Portland, Oregon.* $10-20 each

Tea Kettles

Advertisement showing teakettles in colored aluminum by West Bend, from *Better Homes & Gardens,* October 1952. The ad refers to anodized aluminum as "Electro-finished." Also pictured at bottom is the familiar penguin server, which has been seen in copper-toned colored aluminum with plastic handles.

Color aluminum tea kettle, marked "Mirro."
$5-10

Tea kettles: (left) Sears Maid of Honor; (right) Revere Ware. $10-15 (Sears); $5-10 (Revere)

Tea Kettles: (left) "Comet the Popular Aluminum" with enameled porcelain handle and knob; (center) "Magnalite" by Wagner with wood handle; (right) marked "Mirro." *All pieces courtesy the collection of David Kohl, Portland, Oregon.*
$8-10 (Comet); $10-15 (Magnalite); $6-8 (Mirro)

Tea kettles: (left) Revere Ware; (right) West Bend. $5-10 each

Descoware and Druware

World War II had halted the import of almost everything from overseas (except war footage and misery). "Buy American" was the theme of the times. However, with the end of war came the return of imported items. Everything from paper Chinese lanterns to French perfume was suddenly available again (and import tax was still low). Two porcelain enamel cast iron cookware lines arrived on our shores and made a big impression.

One, called Descoware, was from Belgium. Descoware came in yellow, orange, or a combination of the two, as well as a few other odd choices like blue. Frying pans and casseroles are most often found.

The other line is called Druware and was made in Holland. Druware came in three colors: pastel blue, green, or yellow. The sparse decorations include a few hand-painted tulips and the like. The collection you see in this book started when my mother received a set of skillets, some saucepots, and a large kettle for a wedding present in 1949. Since then I have found some incredible pieces, with much searching. Desco and Dru must have been slightly more upscale pieces and there certainly wasn't anything else like them at the time that I'm aware of. I do see pieces of Desco at thrift stores today, but most of it is pretty decimated. Notice the two "go-along" ceramic Dru pieces. I'm sure there are more!

Druware tea kettle, rare.
$25-40

Druware casseroles in yellow, two sizes, oval.
$20-30 each

Druware round covered casseroles in blue, two sizes.
$20-30 each

Druware round 6" bakers in blue.
$10-15

Druware casserole in blue, oval.
$20-30

Large Druware saucepans, two
sizes, in yellow and blue.
$20-30 each

Druware: (top) saucepan in green; (bottom) 7" skillet in green. $10-15 (saucepan); $8-12 (skillet)

Druware: three-section baker with lid in green. Unusual. $25-30

Druware: (left) three-piece butterwarmer in green; small casserole in green; ceramic "go-alongs" — a cruet and small baker in blue. $10-15 (butterwarmer); $8-12 (casserole); $4-8 each (go-alongs)

Druware open roaster in yellow, oval. $15-20

Teflon

The era of cookware and appliances in this book draws to a close with the introduction of Teflon to American kitchens. Teflon's appearance coincided with a stylistic change that made kitchenware design totally different in the 1960s. Colors like Harvest Gold, Suede, and Avocado were more in demand for appliances and cookware than chrome and Bakelite.

Teflon was discovered around 1938 by scientists working on flourocarbon refrigerants for DuPont Chemical Company. They discovered a new gas that, when compressed, changed to a white solid that felt something like a bar of wet soap. This flourocarbon resin plastic was Polytetraflouroethylene (PFE), later given the trade name "Teflon" by Dupont. Under severe tests it was noted that hardly anything would stick to it. It survived exposure to virtually every chemical, moisture did not affect it, and a soldering iron could not melt it.

Teflon was first used during World War II for its heat-resistant and insulating properties. Then, not much was heard of this new "miracle" product until 1953, when in *Science News Letter* reports that Mr. L. W. Cornell, development engineer of the Minnesota Mining and Manufacturing Company, stated that more and more commercial bakeries and large kitchens were finding Teflon-coated equipment to their liking. Teflon-coated cookware for home use was still a while off. In 1955, the Selenized Process Company of Omaha, Nebraska announced their "Selinization" process. This process was to be applied to cooking utensils to make them "food-sticking proof" and would be available to the public by 1956. It was not until 1960, though, that American housewives got their first Teflon pieces—in the form of frying pans imported from European companies, of all places. Soon followed the U.S. companies. After some resistance by the buying public and much testing, Teflon-coated cookware and appliances became widely accepted by 1965.

Popular color names were Black, Brown, Steel Blue, Lite Green, and Sand. Teflon was applied to all types of cookware and bakeware, as well as appliances like the electric frypan and waffle iron. Two coats were sprayed and the baked on.

Early Teflon struggled with one of its greatest liabilities—it scratched easily. People worried about pieces chipping off into their food. Much time was spent reading articles in women's magazines instructing families how to use "non-stick" cookware. Over the years, science has refined TFE into a denser and more durable product, though it still scratches if you use metal or sharp objects in it. Why? Because it is a plastic with the same inertia as glass, both of which scratch very easily. Use wooden, plastic, or Teflon-coated utensils and don't scrub your Teflon kitchenware with anything abrasive. Early Teflon coating was also reported to have scorched from overheating. This was probably true, but also due to the fact that people were cooking as if they were using non-Teflon items. Teflon heats and cooks at a lower flame. Many early pieces were destroyed this way.

Collecting Teflonware? Good luck! This stuff is pretty well decimated whenever you come upon it. Also, since it is still being made, you have to know the old from the new. It is challenging! I can't say these pieces are impossible to find—I have a Teflon-coated muffin tin in its original plastic bag dated 1964, and a friend has an aluminum saucepan with Teflon-coated egg poaching inserts he bought new in 1967!

Egg poacher with Teflon-coated inserts in avocado color, marked "Wear-Ever," mid-1960s. *Courtesy of Jim Sutherland.*
$5-10

Instruction booklet showing Teflon-coated frying pan, circa 1962.

Bibliography

Celehar, Jane A. *Kitchens and Kitchenware.* Lombard, IL.: Wallace Homestead, 1985.

Cherne, Leo. *The Rest of Your Life.* New York: Doubleday, Doran & Co., 1944.

"Every Crafted Toaster Pops Up," *The Oregonian.* Portland, OR: Sunday, March 20, 1994.

Forty, Adrian. *Objects of Desire.* New York: Pantheon Books, 1986.

Fredgant, Don. *Electric Collectibles.* San Luis Obispo, CA: Padre Productions, 1981

Friday, Franklin. *A Walk Through the Park: The History of GE Appliances and Appliance Park.* Louisville, KY: Elfun Historical Society, 1987.

Fusco, Tony. *The Official Identification and Price Guide to Art Deco.* New York: House of Collectibles, 1988.

Garshman, Barbara J. "Graniteware," *Collectibles.* Spring 1995.

Jorgensen, Janice, ed. *Encyclopedia of Consumer Brands Vol 3.* Detroit; London; Washington, D.C.: Saint James Press, 1994.

Lisfshey, Earl. *The Housewares Story.* Chicago: National Housewares Manufacturers Association, 1973.

Parr, James Gordon. *Man, Metals, and Modern Magic.* Cleveland, OH: American Society for Metals, 1958.

Rombauer, Irma, *Joy of Cooking.* Indianapolis/New York: Bobbs-Merrill Co., 14th Edition 1979.

The World Book Encyclopedia. Chicago, IL: A Scott Fetzer Co., 1993.

Wright, Mary and Russel. *Mary and Russel Wright's Guide to Easier Living.* New York: Simon and Schuster, 1951.

Advertisement for a blender by Hamilton Beach, from *Good Housekeeping,* May 1954.

Advertisement for "Iona Blend" blender by Iona Mfg. Co., from
Good Housekeeping, December 1958.